The Fictional Art of ARUN JOSHI

An Existential Perspective

VACHASPATI DWIVEDI

ATLANTIC
PUBLISHERS & DISTRIBUTORS

Published by
ATLANTIC PUBLISHERS AND DISTRIBUTORS
B-2, Vishal Enclave, Opp. Rajouri Garden, New Delhi-27
Phones : 25413460, 25429987, 25466842

Sales Office
7/22, Ansari Road, Darya Ganj, New Delhi-110 002
Phones : 23273880, 23275880, 23280451
Fax : 91-11-23285873
web : www.atlanticbooks.com
e-mail : info@atlanticbooks.com

ISBN 81-269-0382-1

Printed in India at
Nice Printing Press, Delhi

Preface

Arun Joshi is one of the perceptive contemporary Indian English novelists who have attempted to grapple with the predicament of modern man in their writings. While Anita Desai and Kamala Markandaya concentrate on the social scenario and endeavour to underline its inadequacies, Joshi explores the individual psyche of the protagonists. Imbued with an instinctive urge to define their identity in relation to themselves, to their society and also to humanity at large, his heroes take plunge into the extremely trying situations and combat with them in their peculiar ways. Though influenced by the Western Existentialism, Joshi appropriates his response and answers from the native soil.

Man's spiritual quest may take several forms with Joshi's protagonists. Despite surrounded by affluence and sophistication, they mark themselves as 'outsiders,' misfits in an apparently satisfactory environment of materialistic age where something invaluable—'the deeper poise of the spirit'—is missing. The search for values which could serve as cornerstones of faith and conviction tosses them from one alternative to another leaving them battered and emaciated. This exploration is not a smooth and easy process and has its scars and bruises. The agonising experience culminates in resolving the tension, though implicit and far fetched it might appear. His technique of self-introspection intensified by self-mockery of the protagonists opens a new dimension in post-independence Indian English fiction. It is because of his novel approach, his psychological understanding of the inner conflict of human beings and his existential vision that one is enamoured to his writings.

The conflict between human self and his environment has often baffled human existence. It has given birth to different varieties of fiction through which writers have tried to analyse the anxiety and absurdity of human situations. Right from his first novel Joshi is deeply involved in the "exploration of the mysterious underworld, which is the human soul, and its lonely journey through a world where it is necessarily a stranger, a foreigner" (Mathai: 8).

In *The Strange Case of Billy Biswas,* his second novel, he writes that "life's meaning lies not in the glossy surfaces of our pretentions, but in those dark mossy labyrinths of the soul that languish forever" (Joshi, 1971: 56) and "my novels are essentially attempts towards a better understanding of the world and of myself" (Bannerjee: 3). These statements reveal Joshi's deep interest in delineating and interrogating human situation in this world of cybernetics through his five novels namely *The Foreigner* (1968), *The Strange Case of Billy Biswas* (1971), *The Apprentice* (1974), *The Last Labyrinth* (1981) and *The City and The River* (1990), besides a collection of short stories—*The Survivor* (1975). The present work intends to analyse the spiritual odyssey of Arun Joshi's protagonists and also the stylistic strategies employed by him to articulate their anguish. The work consists of 6 chapters followed by the 'Final Estimate' of the novelist on the whole.

The first section of the opening chapter 'Introduction' is devoted to a survey of the social, economic and political situation obtaining in the 20th century and the development of Indian English fiction. It also takes into account the change that came in Indian English fiction after Independence when the authors shifted their focus from the public to the private sphere. The achievements of contemporary Indian novelists like Anita Desai, Kamala Markandaya and Chaman Nahal have also been taken note of with a view to juxtaposing their appreciation of reality with Joshi's. It also focuses on the existential human situation which acquired greater poignancy and seriousness after the Second World War. The concluding section of this chapter titled 'The Making of The Artist's Sensibility', deals with the biographical details of the novelist, significant events of his life and also his exposure to the outside world. The literary and non-literary influences such as *The Bhagwadgita, The Upanishads, Vedanta,* Albert Camus, Sartre, Kierkegaard, Karl Jaspers, Gabriel Marcel and others have been discussed as well to reach a comparative study of the Hindu vision and modern existential vision. Owing to Joshi's inter-disciplinary predilections, the quality of these experiences, peripheral or otherwise, have also been ascertained with the help of illustrative citations.

After the Introduction, with a view to ensure an indepth study, Joshi's oeuvre has been analysed in five substantive chapters. The second chapter, 'Redemption Through Action: *The Foreigner,'* is devoted to the study of Joshi's *magnum opus, The Foreigner.* The novel enacts the crisis of the present age in the person of Sindi Oberoi, the narrator hero, who feels like a foreigner everywhere. He is a perennial outsider, an uprooted young man whose rootlessness is not merely one of geography or nationality, it is rooted within his soul from which he can't free himself until he comes to India and meets a *Karmyogi* in the person of Muthu, a labourer who teaches him the reality lying beneath the apparent chaos (*Maya*) of the world. Sindi learns that one's life is meaningful only when it is of some use to others and like a *Karmyogi,* Sindi surrenders himself to the upliftment of the deprived and poor labourers around him.

Joshi's second novel, *The Strange Case of Billy Biswas* has been critically examined in the third chapter, 'Redemption Through Action: *The Strange Case of Billy Biswas.'* It develops the theme of anxiety and alienation more effectively than the first novel but with a mystical taste. Billy comes from the upper crust of Indian society with all claims of aristocracy but Billy is never at ease in it. The later events of the novel show how the mystical urge "a strange *urkraft*" (Joshi, 1971: 19) in Billy forces him to shun his family and go to the tribals in Maikala hills to feel a sense of belonging in the real sense. It is in the primitive world he finds his identity. When certain external forces try to uproot him, he prefers to die rather than return to the degenerating modern civilization. The novel stands as a bitter commentary on the tyranny of the phoney metropolitan civilization which crushes man's desire for self-existence and kinship with Nature.

The fourth chapter of this book, 'Redemption Through Devotion: *The Apprentice*' deals with Joshi's 3rd novel *The Apprentice*. It depicts the plight of Ratan Rathor caught in the pangs of guilt and confession, after having lived a life filled with perfidy, chicanery, cowardice and corruption. Being a child of double inheritence—the patriotic idealism of his father and the worldly wisdom of his mother—Ratan feels that his life has resulted into "a pile of dung" (Joshi, 1974: 133) in spite of all its pomp and show of material comforts. He exposes his hypocrisy, lying, and womanising through self-mockery as well as his act of clearing the defective war materials that have led to the death of the Brigadier, his only friend. After such realisation, Ratan accepts penance as the only way to seek peace, consolation and moral courage. He begins with dusting the shoes at the stairs of the temple with humility with the hope for self purification.

Joshi's Sahitya Academy Award winning title *The Last Labyrith* has been analysed in the 5th chapter entitled 'Dilemma of a Doubting Thomas: *The Last Labyrinth.'* It probes into the turbulent inner world of the narrator hero who is relentlessly driven by undefined hungers. The thematic structure of the novel concentrates upon two things "hungers of the body" and "hungers of the spirit" (Joshi, 1981: 11) and it is suggested that man is torn between divers pulls of these. Due to his skeptical approach Som Bhaskar fails to have any understanding of the spirit on the metaphysical side and thus falls a victim to lust (*Kama)* and other vices such as wrath, greed and pride. When man becomes blind with desire, the path of salvation (*Moksha*) becomes illusive to him and he finds himself in a labyrith. Som's skeptical approach to God makes him a perfect example of doubting Thomases who stumble and fall in their life as stated by Lord Krisna in *The Bhagvadgita.* It is apparent that the novel has a religious background and suggests that man's affirmation is possible only through faith and right action.

The fifth and last novel, *The City and The River* has been analysed in the 6th chapter of this work entitled 'The Ultimate Reality: *The City and The River.'* Joshi's last novel is a macrocosm of whatever Joshi has written in his earlier novels. The existential questions put forth to Sindi Oberoi, Billy Biswas, Ratan Rathor and Som Bhaskar are asked this time to whole humanity symbolised by the City depicted in the novel and it has to choose between "allegiance to God" and "allegiance to Man" (Joshi, 1994: 21). It has a fairly vast canvas and deals with the relation of man with other men, with Nature and with God and the progress of mankind from creation to disintegration. The novel strikes an alarm to us by the fate of the City when it is destroyed in the end—a storm rises, the sky turns black, the river swells and turning into an irrepressible ocean and sweeps all—the powerful rulers and everything for the creation of a new city with its new people.

The last section, 'Overall Evaluation' places Joshi in the comity of contemporary novelists who have delved deeper into sensitive psyche of their characters and it contains the findings that I have reached at. The unmistakable impression that finally emerges from a careful observation of Joshi's novels demonstrates that the human situation is his greatest priority. He seems to be convinced of the fact that the Hindu existential vision is the only solution to human problems. With the rapidly growing value crisis and its unfortunate repercussions in the present age of cybernetics, the need for spiritual concerns is all the more pronounced. The significance of Joshi's creative output lies not simply in the number of volumes he has brought out, but the quality of their authentic responses to dilemmas that have been baffling humanity since the Fall.

It is my privilege to place on record my deep sense of gratitude to my teacher Prof. Surya Nath Pandey, (Head, Department of English, B.H.U.) whose continuous guidance, coaxing and encouragement enabled me to complete this work. But for his invaluable suggestions, I might not have been able to reach this stage. I am also thankful to Prof. R.K. Shukla, Prof. N.K. Lal, Prof. R.N. Rai, Prof. M.S. Pandey (Department of English, B.H.U.) and Prof. G. Rai (Department of English, D.D.U. Gorakhpur University) for their help and advice from time to time. I owe a great debt to my parents and other members of my family whose unending love and blessings have been greatest strength in my life.

VACHASPATI DWIVEDI

Contents

1

INTRODUCTION

Arun Joshi is a major contemporary Indian English novelist who has attempted to grapple with the predicament of modern man. While Mulk Raj Anand, R.K. Narayan and Raja Rao concentrate, by and large, on the social scenario in the native country and endeavour to underline its inadequacies, Joshi's main thrust is on the individual psyche of the protagonist. Imbued with an instinctive urge to define their identity in relation to themselves, to their society and also to humanity at large, Joshi's heroes plunge into the extremely trying situations and combat with them in their peculiar and distinctive ways. Despite surrounded by affluence and sophistication, they mark themselves as 'outsiders,' as misfits in the apparently satisfying environment where something more valuable—'the deeper poise of the spirit'—is missing. The search for values which could serve as cornerstones of faith and affirmation tosses them from one alternative to another leaving them batterred and emaciated. This exploration is not a smooth and easy process and has its own obvious scars and bruises. However, the agony of the protagonists culminates in resolving the tension, though implicit and far-fetched at times it might appear. By virtue of such existential themes and a skilful weaving of fictional techniques in his novels, Joshi has created an enviable space for himself in the comity of Indian novelists. Joshi has to his credit five novels and a collection of short stories which have yet to receive the critical attention they deserve. Before undertaking an indepth study of Arun Joshi's works, it is imperative to peruse the beginnings of Indian English fiction to appreciate him in its proper perspective.

Indian English literature is a body of writing which is the creation of Indian race responding fruitfully to the Western impact during the 19th and 20th centuries of colonial period. Though English was first introduced to de-orientalise and anglicise India, it set the stage for a complete intellectual and cultural regeneration of Indian society and opened the floodgates of Western ideas. This exposure brought the dormant intellectual and critical impulse into sudden life and manifested itself in social, religious and political awareness. It also induced a creative urge in the intellectuals like Raja Ram Mohan Roy, Henry Louis Vivian Deorozio, Kashi Prasad Ghose and Micheal Madhusudan Dutt among others and this phase is often termed as the renaissance of modern Indian English literature.

By resorting to a liberal and creative use of English language Ram Mohan Roy ushered in a new epoch of English literature. His articles were published in *The Hindu, The Statesman* and *The Times of India* and built up excellent standards in English and cultivated a public taste by the popularity they enjoyed among the educated classes. After him it was Henry Vivian Derozio who contributed a lot in the fruition of Indian English literature. Born of an Indian Mother and a Portuguese father, he started his career as a teacher of English literature at Hindu College, Calcutta. As a poet, he was influenced by the Romantics notably Byron, Scott, Moore, Shelly and Keats and wrote many poems in the love of his country and Nature. Kashi Prasad Ghose was one of the first Indians to publish a regular volume of English verse, *The Shair and Other Poems* (1830). Ghose was educated at Hindu College and had edited an English weekly *The Hindu Intelligence* as well. Michael Madhusudan Dutt was comparatively more talented than Kashi Prasad Ghose. Though Dutt's fame now rests on his great Bengali epic, *Meghanad Badha* but he had also written many essays, verses and dramas. His narrative poem *The Captive Ladie* (1849) demonstrates the influence of English romantic poets on him. The contributions of these intellectuals brought many social reforms and inculcated a questioning spirit for national freedom besides accelerating the expansion of English in several parts of the country. In the field of literature, however, their endeavours were limited only to essays, articles, poems and translations rooted in the urge of national reconstruction. This trend is also revealed in the works of some other intellectuals like Keshab Chandra Sen, Kashinath Tailang and Dadabhai Nairoji. It is significant to note that the years between 1818 and 1850 witnessed the emergence of prose as well as the appearance of journals and periodicals in most of the Indian languages which became a sound base for the rise of the novel in the eighteen sixties.

It was in the later half of the nineteenth century that writers like Bankim Chandra Chatterjee, Toru Dutt and Romesh Chandra Dutt attempted to give the Indian English novel its real beginning. Bankim Chandra Chatterjee wrote *Rajmohan's Wife* (1864) and it became the first Indian English novel which set the stage for the emergence of novel as a form of literary expression in India. It was followed by *Durgeshnandini* in Bengali which appeared in an English translation in 1890. *Kapala Kundala, Vishavriksha, Anandamath, Devi Chaudharani* and other novels appeared between 1866 and 1880. In *Poison Tree*, which is the translation of *Vishavriksha*, a married man starts loving a young widow and there is great hue and cry. The sad plight of a widow in Hindu society was another recurrent motif in Indian fiction besides the theme of national freedom which is dealt in Bankim's best novel, *Anandamath*. This work comprises the well-known song *Bandemataram* which taught people the gospel of patriotism and influenced the artists all over India. Bankim's real contribution to the development of the Indian fiction in English is that he adapted an alien form and medium to a theme which was essentially Indian and never became a slave to the western tradition of story telling in his novels by seeking a reconciliation between the two views of life. Though *Rajmohan's Wife* cannot be considered a remarkable novel but it did inaugurate a long series of novels to come. Raj Lakshmi Devi wrote *The Hindu Wife* (1876) and it was followed by Toru Dutt's unfinished novel *Bianca* or *The Young Spanish Maiden* (1878), Kali Krishna Lahiri's *Roshanara* (1881), H. Dutt's *Bijoy Chand* (1888) and Kshetrapal Chakravarti's *Sarata And Hingana* (1895). Romesh Chandra Dutt wrote all his novels in

Bengali but translated two of them into English, *The Lake of Palms* (1902) and *The Slave Girl of Agra* (1909). His later three novels, *Todar Mall, Shivaji* and *Pratap Singh* were translated into English by his son. All these novels, either written or translated in English shaped the reader's interest and motivated many a later writers to choose—the long sustained piece of prose fiction—as their creative medium.

As a great writer, Bankim Chandra Chatterjee remained an inspiration throughout his life for many later novelists and poets such as Rabindra Nath Tagore and Sarat Chandra Chatterjee disposed to the cause of national freedom and social reconstruction. Tagore is the most outstanding figure in Bengali literature and it was his *Gitanjali* which won the Nobel Prize for literature in 1912. Though he is known as a great poet all over the world he was also a novelist of no less significance. The success of *Gitanjali* gave a boost to translations and publications of his Bengali writings in English as well as in other languages. Of Tagore's full-length novels, only three appeared in approved English versions in his life time. *Naukadubi* (1905) appeared as *The Wreck, Gora* (1910) retained the same title, and *Ghare Bahire* (1916) became *The Home and The World* but his first success was *Choker Bali* (1902) which was translated into English by Krishna Kriplani as *Binodini.* It deals with the plight of a young widow and presents a deep psychological study of its characters. By the ideas that work in the novel, Tagore affirms the right of the widow to be married, to be free and to get love from the society in the place of neglect and suppression. *Gora* projects the vision of Tagore regarding the individual in renascent India. The hero, Gora, grows up as an orthodox Hindu in the care of his foster parents Krishnadayal and Anandmoyi and it is later on that he realises that his mother was an Irish who had died after giving birth to him. The readers' opinion is divided between Gora and Suchitra and their love is shown in conflict with religious orthodoxy which makes the novel a play of ideas. *The Home and The World* has the background of revolutionary Bengal of 1905 when the atmosphere was in turmoil with slogans of 'Swadeshi' and 'Bandemataram' and the novel is the artistic presentation of the impact of these nationalist forces on the life of individuals like Nikhil, an idealistic husband, his wife Bimal, and his friend, Sandeep.

Sarat Chandra Chatterjee contributed his novels in the same style as Bankim and Tagore. His masterpiece *Srikanta* was translated into English by K.C. Sen and Theodosia Thompson. Throughout his novels, Sarat Chandra identified himself with the cause of the down-trodden and boldly portrayed the tears and agonies of the lower, middle and have-not classes. The piercing realism of Sarat Chandra's novels inspired many later writers such as Mulk Raj Anand, R.K. Narayan, Bhabani Bhattacharya, Manohar Malgaonkar, Kamala Markandaya, Khushwant Singh and a few others who have depicted Indian life in all its socio-cultural, economic and political complexities advocating the cause of the down-trodden.

After Sarat Chandra, it is Mulk Raj Anand (b. 1905) who has proved himself to be the most socially-conscious in the long array of later Indian novelists. Born in a traditional coppersmith family in Peshawar, Anand had his education at Lahore, London and Cambridge and took a Doctorate in Philosophy. In spite of his academic achievements, he chose to be a writer and the "advocate of the down-trodden and the underprivileged" (Iyengar: 335). Anand was deeply moved by the Gandhian movement for Harijan uplift and as a serious response he articulated his compassion for the outcastes in his novels. He seems to be deeply influenced by Ruskin, Balzac, Tolstoy, Dickens, Tagore and Premchand throughout in his novels. There are several novels to his credit: *Untouchable, Coolie, Two Leaves and a Bud, The Village, Across The Black Waters, The Sword And The Sickle, The Big Heart, Private Life of An Indian Prince, The Old Woman and The Cow, The Road, Seven Summers* and *The Morning Face.* In almost all the novels Anand has been realistic and naturalistic in his descriptions about the status of the pariahs and untouchables in Indian situation.

Among his novels, *Untouchable* is the most compact piece but exceptionally it is the most revealing also. It covers the events of a single day in the life of a low caste boy, Bakha, in the town of Bulashah. He lives with his father Lakha and sister

Sohini. By the depiction of a single day in the life of Bakha, Anand's able hands underline Bakha's suffering and humiliation at the hands of high caste people as well as the poverty, squalor, ignorance and superstition in Indian society. Iyengar's comment about Anand's dexterity in providing the force of detail and realistic characterisation is quite perceptive:

> *Untouchable* strikes us as the picture of a place, of a society and of certain persons not easily to be forgotten: a picture that is also an indictment of the evils of a decadent and perverted orthodoxy (*Ibid*: 339).

Anand's second novel *Coolie* is a character novel and the action expands over some years and moves through several villages and towns. The hero is Munoo, a young orphan lad who is unfortunate to work as a servant in different households in different towns—Bilaspur-Shamnagar-Daulatpur-Bombay and finally at Shimla—where he dies of consumption. Wherever Munoo goes, he suffers exploitation and his life becomes a macrocosm of India where patient sufferance is the only way left for the poor to survive. His third novel *Two Leaves and a Bud* depicts the tragic life of Gangu, a labourer in Macpherson Tea Estate of Assam, his wife Sajani and their children, Leela and Buddhu. The exploitation of the labourers by the British as well as many Indians has been shown by Anand which ultimately ends in the murder of Gangu by Riggie Hunt, the Assistant Manager who is a living image of cruelty and lust. The next batch of three novels, *The Village, Across The Black Waters* and *The Sword and The Sickle* form a trilogy and deal with the boyhood, youth and early manhood of Lalu Singh, the youngest son of a sikh farmer. Lalu's liking for the primordial life of the village—his enlisting as a sepoy in British Army—his father's death—his visit to France to take part in the First World War—his return to India—his involvement in politics and the clash of ideologies—all these are the contents of these novels. The next work, *The Big Heart* stands very much similar to *Untouchable* thematically but the issue is not between the pariahs and the higher castes, but between *thatheras* (coppersmiths) and the capitalists as their factories have thrown many of them out of employment. Ultimately the capitalists win the game and the old order is replaced by the new. *The Private Life of An Indian Prince* characterises an Indian prince Victor who represents all those *maharajas* and *nawabs* who found themselves nowhere after Independence. Victor leads a luxurious life and has many affairs with women but like many others, he is forced to sign the agreement of Accession. As an after effect, he goes mad and enters an asylum and the novel ends there. Throughout the novel Anand's aim is to fuse the contemporary political history with personal history of a few individuals. In the later novels, *The Old Woman and The Cow, The Road, Seven Summers* and *The Morning Face,* however, Anand deals with humanity and compassion instead of disgust and anger against the social evils but he has done a lot to prove himself a committed writer like Dickens who lets his characters live and speak and act so that they represent their whole lot with vitality.

R.K. Narayan (b. 1907) is a novelist of the middle classes. Born and brought up in a south Indian Hindu middle class family, Narayan shares their beliefs and superstitions and draws from his personal experience the characters and situations of the Indian middle class engaged in a struggle to free themselves from the clutches of the past. He is mainly concerned with the character analysis of the individuals with a comic view of life. College boys, college and school teachers, tourists, guides, merchants, municipal members, taxi-drivers of Malgudi (an imaginary place like Thomas Hardy's Wessex) are the familiar characters we meet in his novels. Throughout Narayan's novels, there is a disturbance of order in the beginning followed by a return and then a restoration of normalcy at Malgudi. In his first novel *Swami And Friends,* Malgudi is a town of modest size and as we pass over other novels, they show us an advance in time at Malgudi. The other remarkable thing is the transmigration of his characters from novel to novel. In *Bachelor of Arts* Krisna takes the place of Swami. He falls in love with a girl but is not allowed to marry her because their horoscopes do not match. Out of frustration, he renounces the world and becomes a *sadhu,* only to run away later on when he is taken to be one. Finally, he finds happiness in marrying a girl he has not seen and by falling in love with her. In *The Dark Room,* the proud heroine, Savitri, after discovering her husband's infidelity, sulks and goes to the dark room, *i.e., 'Kop Bhawan'*. Later on she abandons her husband and children, but after being tormented by the memories of her children returns to her household. The work is an ironical social comedy of the husband Ramani's uneasy affair with his children to keep them amused and taking them daily to Palace Talkies. *The English Teacher* completes the trilogy begun by *Swami and Friends* and *The Bachelor of Arts* and the novel depicts Krishna's married life with Sushila, her years of illness to her death and Krishna's journey to the cremation ground, all this is written in a very moving way. *Waiting For the Mahatma* stands as an exception because its action extends as far as Delhi from Malgudi and it describes the Bharati-Sriram romance which attains a new scope due to their indulgence in politics and their common allegiance to the Mahatma. In the last group of novels, *Mr. Sampath, The Financial Expert, The Guide, The Man Eater of Malgudi* and *The Sweet Vendor*, Narayan's art reaches its perfection. *The Guide* which won the Sahitya Akademi Award in 1960, depicts Raju, its protagonist as a romantic young man like his predecessors Margaya (*The Financial Expert*) and Sampath (*Mr. Sampath*) and plays many parts—guide of Marco—lover of Rosie and Mahatma through the novel and at last, he undertakes a twelve day fast to end a drought during which he reveals to his chief disciple Velan, the whole truth about himself. On the last day of his fast, he dies a martyr. *The Man Eater of Malgudi* presents H. Vasu, M.A. Taxidermist and with him we are back in Malgudi and the nearby Mempi hills, its tea-shop, the village temple and Kumara, the ailing elephant. The novel is the modern version of the *Dev-Asura* conflict and Bhasmasur myth of Indian mythology. *The Sweet Vendor* renders the chasm between Jagan, the father, and Mali, his son. Jagan is a small businessman professing asceticism whereas his son Mali is given to greed and materialism. Mali goes to America and returns with Grace, a girl who is half Korean and half American. The discovery of Jagan that his son is living with a woman to whom he is not married shatters the old morals and values of the middle classes in India. The novel beautifully exposes both, the father, a conservative conformist and the son, a modern, unthinking rebel. Narayan's portrayal of the Indian life with unusual ease and dexterity provided model for later artists.

Raja Rao (b. 1908) completes the triad of these novelists who shaped Indian English novel and canonised it as an important component of Commonwealth Literature. Rao has been greatly influenced by Gandhian revolution as manifested in his works. His first novel *Kanthapura* presents life seen through a believer's perspective. India, like Sita is in the grip of Ravana—like British. Gandhi is depicted as the *avatar* of Vishnu to save India from the 'Redmen'. Moorty is the local hero, a Gandhian leader. All political education is conveyed through the *harikatha* man, Jayaramachar who retells the Rama epic equating it with Gandhi's struggle for *Swaraj*. Moorty, the hero of the novel is balanced by the villain, Bade Khan, the policeman who is the symbol of oppression and represents soulless bureaucracy of the British. His second novel, *The Serpent and The Rope* is dominated mostly by Indian philosophy and cultural legacy. Raja Rao's protagonist Rama (Ramaswami) is haunted by the teachings of Shankara about *Advaita Vedanta* which teaches that there is only one reality in existence, the idea of *Brahman-Atman* and God. The other identities are mere illusions, born of man's ignorance, *Ajnana*. When we think all that as real, we are like men in the dark who mistake a rope for a serpent. Ramaswamy's marriage with Madeleine, his craving for spiritual knowledge and his quest for his own identity in France and later in India make him a real sage reaching his self-recognition. Using the familiar analogy of the serpent and the rope, Rama states the well-known *advaita* position with regard to the ultimate reality of *Brahma*. The beauty of the novel lies in depicting the tortuous mind of a cultivated Indian who is caught between the ambiguous agonising present and his ancient cultural legacy. His third novel, *Cat And Shakespeare* (1965) is a novel experiment by Raja Rao who calls it 'a metaphysical comedy'. Both 'Cat' and 'Shakespeare' are symbols and the reader has to infer a great deal to read between the lines. By enacting a kind of surrender to destiny and God through the characters Govindan Nair and Pai, the novel suggests Rao's conception of human life. His other novel *Comrade Kirillov* reads like an extended character sketch. The protagonist Kirillov is an Indian intellectual with his rather eccentric opinions on communism, the British, and Indian freedom struggle. He is viewed with good humoured irony as a professed communist who is yet very much Indian. Rao's latest novel *The Chessmaster and His Moves* is the first part of an ambitious trilogy, the second and the third parts of which are yet to be published. Extremely philosphical in content as usual, it centres in Rao's obsessive problem and its attendant complexities. His recourse to the ethos of the Gandhian era, *Vedanta* and Metaphysics makes his claim to be called a thoroughly Indian novelist who wishes Indians not to look towards the Western civilization but to derive sustenance from their own culture which is no less enlightening.

The women novelists who succeeded this trio include Kamala Markandaya (b. 1924), Ruth Prawer Jhabwala (b. 1927) and Nayantara Sahgal (b. 1927) who have shown a stern consistency of purpose in writing novels. Kamala Markandaya's novel attempt to present the change that has been taking place in Indian scene in the wake of materialism. The conflict between a nostalgic idealism of traditional values and a new compulsive urge for modernity is a focal theme in her novels. *Nectar in a Sieve,* her first novel captures this dichotomy of values in a forceful manner through the life of peasants and a housewife like Rukmini. *Some Inner Fury* presents an Indian caught up in the maelstorm of her struggle against the British while *A Silence of Desire* brings into sharp focus another aspect of the conflict between tradition and change. Here she is essentially concerned with the tension between faith and reason, spiritualism and rationalism. In *Possession* she attempts another variation on the theme of acquisition and egocentrism through Lady Caroline Bell, a rich divorcee and Valmiki, an amateur artist whom she wants to possess. *A Handful of Rice* portrays the milieu of Indian city life in which Ravi, fresh from a village, feels confused to choose between conscience and violence, compassion and cruelty, integrity and cunning. Her other novels, *Coffer Dams, The Nowhere Man, Two Virgins* and *The Pleasure City* carry contemporary relevance as her world is peopled with individuals caught existentially between spiritualism and materialism and if interpreted in terms of tradition and change, her novels acquire a new coherence and meaning.

The novels of Nayantara Sahgal revolve around two main themes—one, that India is changing with time and Indian people should adjust to these changes, and second, that lack of communication between individuals *i.e.*, husband and wife, causes unhappiness and prevents human fulfilment. *This Time of Morning* portrays the upper strata of Indian society and launches Sahgal's theme of isolation of the individual and the need of human understanding. The next novel, *Storm in Chandigarh* begins with politics and grapples with its effect on the life and affairs of its characters. Written with restraint and perception, it depicts man's desire to gain control over other's mind and analyses the deeper layers of human behaviour. *A Day in Shadow* begins where *Storm in Chandigarh* ends. The linear development of theme results in the theme of lack of understanding in man-woman relationship leading to the failure of marriage. It also deals with the attempt of an Indian woman to liberate herself from the moral and social pressures that combine with economic dependence. In her other novels, *A Time to Be Happy, A Situation in New Delhi, Rich Like Us, Plans for Departure,* and *Mistaken Identity,* Sahgal's projection of Indian reality is worked through religion and morality on the one hand, and politics and tradition on the other that are dominated sometimes by economic ethos and sometimes by individual freedom to act according to his/her own conscience.

Jhabwala has to her credit several novels—*To Whom She Will, The Nature of Passion, Esmond in India, The Householder, Get Ready for Battle, A Backward Place, Heat And Dust* and *Three Continents.* She is primarily a writer of domestic comedy and in her earlier novels, Jhabwala is concerned with love and marriage, wife-hunting as well as the involvement of parents in arranging marriages in Indian society, and the various troublesome consequences arising due to unmatched marriage situations. In her later novels, *Heat and Dust* and *Three Continents,* Jhabwala's preoccupation with East and West encounter and the question of identity with Indian ethos creates a conflicting situation for characters. She has poignantly rendered how India is seen by the Western characters when they are forced to be assimilated in the Indian space due to their marriage and love relationships.

Novelists like Bhabani Bhattacharya (b. 1906) and Manohar Malgaonkar (b. 1913) have depicted the Indian society after Independence, its social evils and corruption as well as the suffering inflicted upon people by Second World War and Chinese attack on India. Bhattacharya has published six novels which form rather a valuable achievement—*So Many Hungers, Music for Mohini, He Who Rides a Tiger, A Goddess Named Gold, Shadows from Ladakh,* and *A Dream in Hawaii* and his main object is to present Indian socio-economic scenario with a view to ameliorate it. In his first novel, *So Many Hungers,* the novelist has portrayed the ravages of hunger on an epic scale. The hunger of stomach gives place to the hunger for freedom from the British in *He Who Rides a Tiger.* As one of the character Biten says, the entire story is "a legend of freedom, a legend to inspire and awaken," there are several references to Gandhi and his ideals in the novel. *Shadows from Ladakh* and *A Goddess Named Gold* deal with the question of how a country should make most of its liberation and how its benefits can be passed on to the masses. In *Music for Mohini,* Bhattacharya satirises Indian people for their superstitious, beliefs and customs. In his latest novel, *A Dream in Hawaii,* Bhattacharya treats the theme of integration of values. The novel presents a blending of the old and new values of the East and the West in its principal character, Swami Yogananda. While upholding Indian values, Bhattacharya gives a message of synthesis, accommodation and compromise of traditional and modern values throughout his novels.

The novels of Manohar Malgaonkar, *The Princes, Distant Drum, Combat of Shadows, A Bend in Ganges* and *The Devil's Hand* reveal his interest in the post-Independence scenario and its effect on human life. *The Princes* depicts the prince Abhayaraj struggling to keep up the old order stable even after Independence. Army life and human isolation is the theme of *Distant Drum. Combat of Shadows* presents a sensitive understanding of the relationship between the Anglo-Indians and the British officers in rapidly changing India. Partition of India and the consequent Hindu-Muslim riots are the subject matter of *A Bend in Ganges* whereas *The Devil's Hand* relates the personal history of Nana Saheb. All the novels reflect Malgaonkar's keener perception of life and his artistic integration of history within the framework of fiction. Some other novelists include Khawaja Ahmad Abbas of *Men and Rivers* and *Inquilab*, Sudin N. Ghose who wrote *And Gazelles Leaping, Cradle of the Clouds* and *The Vermilion Boat*, G.V. Desani of the well-known *All About H. Haterr* and Khushwant Singh of *Train to Pakistan, I shall Not Hear the Nightingale* and *Delhi* and Chaman Nahal of *Azadi*.

After 1960s the Indian English fiction, similar to its western counterpart, shifted its focus from the public to the private sphere. The mass destruction in the two World Wars caused by nuclear weapons brought envy, unrest and boredom all over the world. These absurd situations gave rise to psychosocial disorders and loss of moral values in humanity and ultimately disturbed man's mental peace and harmony and brought discomfort, depression and frustration. The world literature, pertaining to these ethos, started to deal with the different gloomy facets of modern society. The Indian novelists, however, could not remain aloof from these currents and henceforth they were not exclusively concerned with the exploration and interpretation of a social milieu and dealt with new subjects of human existence and man's quest for self in all its complicated situations. This shift of focus in Indian English fiction becomes clearer particularly with Arun Joshi and Anita Desai who explore the agonised existence of modern man in their writings.

Anita Desai's *Forte* is the exploration of modern Indian sensibility that is not at ease in the modern set-up and through her novels *Cry, The Peacock* (1963), *Voices in the City* (1965) and *Bye-Bye, Blackbird* (1971), she has added a new dimension to the achievement of Indian women novelists in English fiction. Her first novel, *Cry, The Peacock* is a highly impressionistic account of the incompatible marital life of Maya, a hypersensitive woman who causes her detached and careless husband, Gautam to fall to his death from the roof because he stands between her and a particularly beautiful moonrise. The cry of the peacock symbolises the elusive equipose she aspires for. The title of the novel is appropriate in the context of the protagonist's quest for a rare poise which is not possible in this world. In her second novel, *Voices in the City*, the Maya-Gautam tragedy is re-enacted in Monisha-Jiban marriage and Anita Desai captures eloquently the voices of the spiritual quest of three young people who are sensitive, educated and excessively self-conscious but plagued by the absence of goals in their life in the 'city of death', Calcutta. Nirode, Monisha and Amla wither and waste away their potential. Their desperate cries show variations of their quest for self-discovery and self-realisation at the expense of abandoning the old guides of family, religion, custom and tradition. Similarly, in other novels too, the existential predicament is the *zeit geist* of all the major characters of her novels. Her Akademi Award winner *Where Shall We Go This Summer* deals with Sita's awareness of the basic dichotomy in the urban milieu between compassion in life and the odour of death and destruction, and her resultant urge to free herself from the entire civilization and reach affirmation. In *Clear Light of Day*, Desai draws an ironic parallel between the freedom of the country and Raja's and Bim's own personal freedom. The theme of liberation, freedom and peace acquires new dimensions in Anita Desai's artistic handling in the context of family relationships. Her other works, *Fire on the Mountain, In Custody* and *Fasting, Feasting* deal with similar existential questions tormenting the individuals.

Arun Joshi, like Anita Desai, has recorded modern man's traumas and agonies in his novels with rare competence and gravity. His main thrust is on the individual psyche of the protagonist throughout his five novels. His technique of self-introspection intensified by self-mockery opens a new dimension in the art of Indian English fiction. It is because of his novel approach, his psychological understanding of the inner conflict of human beings and his philosophical existential vision that one is enamoured to his writings.

Arun Joshi was born on 7 July, 1939 at Banaras Hindu University, Varanasi where his father, late Prof. A.C. Joshi was on the science faculty of the University (later on he became the Vice-Chancellor as well). The youngest child of his illustrious parents he had his formal education at Varanasi, Lahore and Jalandhar. After completing his Intermediate courses he got a scholarship from the U.S.A. to pursue higher studies. He obtained a Degree in engineering from the University of Kansas in 1959 and Master's degree in Industrial Management from Massachussets Institute of Technology, U.S.A. in 1960. During his American sojourn, he had also worked at a mental hospital where his uncle was a psychiatrist dealing with chronic schizophrenics for a brief period. After returning to India in 1962, he joined the Delhi Cloth and General Mills Co., Delhi in a managerial capacity, as chief of its Recruitment and Training department. During the later years he worked as the Head of the D.C.M. Corporate Performance Assessment Cell, as Secretary, D.C.M. Board of Management and as Executive Director of Shri Ram Centre for Industrial Relations and Human Resources. In 1964 he was married to Rukmani and had three children—two girls and a boy. He resigned from D.C.M. in 1965 but remained associated with Shri Ram Centre for Art and Culture and Hindu College, Delhi, as a Member of their Governing Bodies. Exceptionally perceptive as a creative artist, Joshi has brought out five novels—*The Foreigner* (1968), *The Strange Case of Billy Biswas* (1971), *The Apprentice* (1974), *The Last Labyrinth* (1981), *The City and The River* (1990) and a collection of short stories, *The Survivor* (1975). He won the prestigious Sahitya Akademi Award for his fourth novel *The Last Labyrinth* in 1982. It was very unfortunate that a man of such amazing abilities died of cardiac arrest in April, 1993 at the age of fifty four in New Delhi.

There are a number of literary and non-literary influences which have their profound impact on Arun Joshi's creative sensibility. The most dominant among them are Hindu scriptures—The *Bhagvadgita*, The *Upanishads, Vedanta*—and Mahatma Gandhi. In his interview with Pier Paolo Piciuco, he accepts that the Hindu tradition has influenced him the most. He candidly seeks his affinity with India:

> I certainly have some affinities with this country [India]; I have found it lately. One is the affinity of the spiritual kind, then there is the affinity of the sensual kind and there are others, too. Each country in India is very unique, and all India still remains unique. You know, historically, India has always been very inner-directed and never outer-directed like many other countries.... There is no other country like this for the religious size, for the spiritual, the Bhakti Movement.... India then has dealings with God which are peculiar. (Piciuco: 89)

Further, Joshi's comment regarding the selection of theme in *The Last Labyrinth* elucidates his stand as a novelist deeply motivated by the Indian view of life: "There is a special Indian viewpoint which I have known all my life" (*Ibid*: 89). Added to these stray realisations, Joshi's ideas regarding divine will, soul, freedom of spirit, detachment, *karmayoga* and God meet the thoughts of Hindu existential thinkers:

> I believe that the soul of man is immortal but there is this Indian belief that the soul is born again and again basically for the evolution of the soul, always under certain conditions. They are where your own life has aligned with the divine will. This is also called *yoga* (*Ibid:* 90).

Later in the same interview he elaborates his concept of individual freedom:

> I guess freedom (or liberty if you like), which is both political and spiritual, I have not much dealt with. But the inner-liberation and the outer-liberation I guess are quite important to me. So inner liberation without detachment is not possible and selfishness is always stopping you from getting liberated. Loneliness is the state where you become aware that you are not liberated and you also do not know how to get liberated. That is the loneliness stage in man's life (*Ibid*: 91).

Joshi is at pains to realize that modern man has lost his faith in God and has become a slave to the money-machine culture. For him, human life is an agonising pilgrimage in which man strives to be an instrument of God. When asked regarding the ways to achieve affirmation in human life, he observes:

> A stage comes in your evolution when you can do without rules. But that person is an instrument of God...there is a long journey before you can reach that stage so that only a few people are inclined to do that. There will be a time again when people will turn towards the divine and want to become instrument of God, rather than living for themselves. They will have problems because it is difficult to judge whether you are instrument of God or not (*Ibid*: 93-94).

All these statements show the deep influence of the *Bhagvadgita, Vedanta* and the *Upanishads* on Joshi's psyche. By employing Indian myths, customs and religious beliefs, Joshi seems to be approximating what C.G. Jung calls the "racial unconscious" or collective unconscious that has been constantly guiding writers like Raja Rao, R.K. Narayan and other Indian writers.

It would be quite pertinent at this stage to linger awhile on the major concerns of the Hindu scriptures, which are at the root of Arun Joshi's creative art. In the philosophy of *Vedanta,* the *Upanishads* and the *Gita,* the most widely discussed subject is the relation between *Brahman* and *Atman. Atman* is individual self whereas *Brahman* represents the Almighty. The highest wisdom that everybody would cherish to attain is to know the self. In the *Upanishads,* human being is never an isolated individual but is related to the Absolute and also to fellow beings as the noted philosopher S. Radhakrishnan comments: "The human being has its root in the invisible though in his life it belongs to the passing stream of the visible" (Radhakrishnan, 1974: 37). The individual souls are different expressions of the One Universal Self, *Brahman.* Though *Brahman* and *Atman* are used interchangeably, the former denotes the substratum of the universe while the latter, the substraum of individual egos. Prajapati in *Chandogya Upanishad* describes the real meaning of the self to Indra:

> Dear Indra! The body is not the self, though it exists for the self.... The self is universal, immanent as well as

> transcendent. The whole universe lives and moves and breathes in it. It is immortal, self-luminous, self proved and beyond doubts and denials, as the very principles which makes all doubts, denials and thoughts possible (Radhakrishnan, 1989: 491).

In another *Upanishad, Brihadaranyaka,* the sage Yajnavalkya declares that the self is the ultimate knower and hence cannot be known as an object because it knows all objects (*Ibid:* 254-55). The relation between *Brahman* and *Atman* (Self) is illustrated in *Swetaswatara Upanishad* as "Two Birds, companions, always united, cling to the self same tree. Of these two one eats the sweet fruit, and the other looks on without eating" (*Ibid:* 733). Here the former is the empirical self and the latter the transcendental self. One who achieves this wisdom is a liberated soul, a perfect sage. The *Bhagvadgita* describes this knowledge of the evolution of the soul essential for a liberated man: "As the soul passes in this body through childhood, youth and age, even so is taking on of another body. The sage is not perplexed by this" (Radhakrishnan, 1993: 104). While the liberated souls know the truth and live in it, the unliberated ones pass from birth to birth, tied by the bondage of works.

Man's access to liberation is through knowledge *(jnana).* It is ignorance (*avidya*) that stands in the way of enlightenment. *Avidya* breeds pride (*ahankar*) and he believes himself to be a separate entity unrelated to *Brahman.* In the *Upanishads,* as well as in Joshi's novels, faith in God is the first step towards man's liberation that exterminates *avidya* and *ahankar*. Much learning also may not be of use unless one has a right disposition. Those who live on the surface of life, may not feel the agony, the denial of spirit and may not have any urge to be liberated. The *Bhagvadgita* calls them *purushapasu* (human animals), but those who realize their dignity as men strive to seek their harmony with the divine will.

The Hindu scriptures describe three different ways to attain the state of liberation and it has been used by Arun Joshi in different novels. These are *Jnanayoga* (a knowledge of the reality), *Bhaktiyoga* (adoration and love of the Supreme Person), and *Karmayoga* (subjection to the will of the Divine purpose).

These can be differentiated on account of the distribution of emphasis on theoretical, emotional and practical purposes due to difference in human dispositions. At the end, knowledge, love and action mingle together. *Jnanayoga* lifts man out of his narrow limits and makes him forget his ego in the contemplation of the universal principles of God. His desires cease and he abstains from indulging in general human weaknesses. The way of devotion (*Bhaktiyoga*) asks for total devotion and the formation of a relationship of trust and love to God. *Bhakti* is to believe in God, to love Him, to be devoted to Him, to enter into Him. Such a devotee has in him the highest knowledge of a perfect man. *Karmayoga* is a mandate for action. At the beginning of *Gita*, Arjuna refuses to fight and asks for abstention of *karma* and retreat from the world. The *Samkhya*, which is another name for *jnana*, requires us to renounce action. It believes that beings are bound by *karma* or action and saved by knowledge. The *Gita* compares both these ideologies and concludes that action (*karma*) is better than renunciation: "The renunciation of works and their unselfish performance both lead to the soul's salvation. But of the two, the unselfish performance of works is better than their renunciation" (*Ibid*: 175). All these three ways of life find their expression in *The Strange Case of Billy Biswas, The Apprentice* and *The Foreigner* respectively.

The concept of *Maya* in Hindu scriptures has also affected Joshi a lot. His protagonists find their life a sort of labyrinth (*bhulbhulaiya*) from which it is difficult to find a way out. *Swetaswatara Upanishad* conceives God as *mayin*, the powerful being who creates the world by His powers. *Maya* is the power of the lord from which the world arises (Radhakrishnan, 1989: 727). The creation has a tendency to delude us into thinking that it is all and the delusive character of the world is *Maya*. The notion of *Maya* has its palpable impact on *The Last Labyrinth*. Joshi brings forth the myth of *sristi* and *pralaya* in his last novel *The City And The River* and suggests man's surrender to the Divine Will as the ultimate solution in the modern world. It is not only the attributes of these philosophies that are present as an undercurrent in Arun Joshi's fiction but even the characters discuss at times various philosophies and philosophers as well. There is also a gradual increase in the philosophical mien from novel to novel.

Among other dominant influences on Joshi's sensibility include the western Existentialist philosophers. In his interview with Purabi Banerjee, Joshi confesses: "I did read Camus and Sartre. I liked *The Plague* and read *The Outsider*. I might have been influenced by them. Sartre I did not understand or like. As for existential philosophers like Kierkegaard, I have never understood except odd statements" (Bannerjee: 4). Like the works of modern existential thinkers, Joshi's novels express the absurdity of man's existence in modern world but they assert their singularity in applying them in the Indian context and deriving solutions from native milieu.

Modern Existentialism, taken as a whole is a philosophical movement of the twentieth century dealing with man's disillusionment and despair in the modern world. When the world was almost torn to pieces by the chaotic conditions caused by the two World Wars, existentialism flourished as a philosophical movement and the existentialist thinkers began to define anxiety, anguish, guilt, dread, despair, death, meaninglessness, etc. of the post-war world in their own ways and achieved a compelling effect on the thought of the literary artists all over the world. Broadly there are three groups of existentialist philosophers—theistic, atheistic and absurdist. Among theistic philosophers, Soren Kierkegaard (1813-1855) is commonly regarded as "the father of modern existentialism, and is the first European philosopher who bears the existentialist label" (Macquarrie: 53). The terms "existence" and "existentialism" were first coined by Kierkegaard himself and by his explanation of existentialism, he brought a revolutionary change in the prevalent political, social and religious ideas in which men were identified by State, society and church. Being a Christian-theistic existentialist, Kierkegaard believed that man acquires self-knowledge only when he has an 'intensified awareness' of God and based his philosophy on the subjectivity of human existence.

Karl Jaspers (1883-1969), a German philosopher, accepts the Kierkegaardian way of faith. He thinks that man in the modern world is doomed to fail though his failure is not always negative. Jaspers talks of "boundary situation" (Jaspers: 23) which is the same as universal situation and man himself is a centre of urges and aversions which either help or obstruct him. Man is thus an existential being because he is subject to chance and fortune, suffering and conflict, guilt and death. Jaspers further elaborates: "The way in which man approaches his failure determines what he will become" (*Ibid.*). He calls existence (things of the world) "dasein" which Kierkegaard terms "being there". According to Jaspers "dasein" is different from "Existenz" which, for him, marks the hidden ground of our thinking and acting and is subjective whereas "existence" is a psychophysical combination or an empirical existence. But man is something more than his empirical existence because he has got freedom to go beyond his present being and has the capacity to establish a communion with other beings. Thus human reality is something more than "existence" or "dasein" and as Jaspers says, "existenz" is the real existence endowed with freedom, choice and determinism.

The French Philosopher, Gabriel Marcel (1889-1973) stated a "metaphysic of hope" and inspired the French people to rediscover their true dignity as human beings. He perceived that the modern man is passing through a very critical phase of modern age. Though he is free, he fails to assert his freedom because of social, political, economic and religious entrapments. He is confused, agonised and depressed. Marcel firmly believed that the ills of our society result from individual's refusal to appeal earnestly to God. In his *The Existential Background to Human Dignity*, he realises that man is a "Homo Viator," always on the way to self-realisation: "I am not, I have to become; I am not free, I have to become free" (Marcel: 169). Man's "Being" is different from "Having" and it is of greater significance. "Having" implies possession and it is an impediment or a burden on human beings whereas "Being" means freedom from these impediments to reach the realm of the realisation of true existence. Marcel's vision has a distrust for supremacy of intellect and it puts stress upon intuition and hope. Hope is a recurring theme of his writings as well as love and it is love through which one actually participates in Being.

The atheistic philosophers, Martin Heidegger and Jean Paul Sartre, are led by Friedrich Nietzsche (1844-1900) who is just opposed to the Kierkegaardian line of argument and proves himself thoroughly anti-Christian and atheist. Through his ideal of "Superman," Nietzsche declares that for the modern man "God is dead" (Nietzsche, 1933: 61). Such a God should be abandoned: "Away with such a God; Better to have no God, better to set up destiny on one's own account, better to be a fool, better to be God oneself" (*Ibid*: 292). He insists that man must exercise his "free choice," his "will" in creating values for his own evolution into a "Superman." This "will" is the most important aspect of all existence and Nietzsche's "Superman" or "Overman" is the expression of man's "will-to-power." The death of God liberates man and imbibes a "genuine consciousness of power and freedom" to project himself as "sovereign individual" (Nietzsche, 1910: 125).

Martin Heidegger's (1889-1976) major work, *Being and Time* presented a thorough analysis of human existence and exerted a profound effect on the later existentialists. Heidegger depicts man in an agonising situation where man's perfection is mere illusion because care, anxiety, guilt, finitude and death shatter his dream of perfection and accomplishment. According to Heidegger there are three fundamental characteristics of existence—"possibility," "factility" and "fallenness" (Heidegger: 57). These three characteristics of the being of man constitute 'care' (*sorge*).

After Heidegger, it is the French intellectual Jean Paul Sartre, a novelist, playwright and philosopher, who is the best known thinker of atheistic existentialism. Like Nietzsche, he believed in the supremacy of man's existence in the godless universe. He proclaims:

> Atheistic existentialism of which I am a representative, declares with greater consistency that if God does not exist there is at least one being whose existence comes before his essence, a being which exists before it can be defined

by any conception of it. That being is man, or as Heidegger has it, the human reality (Sartre, 1955: 124).

In this way in a godless universe man himself has to take the place of God. According to Sartre, there are three kinds of being, an object has "being-in-itself," a man has "being-for-itself," and we all have "being-for-others." Being-in-itself (en-soi) means "non-conscious being" which is what it is. Being-for-itself (pour-soi) means "man's conscious being" which has to be what it is. Being-for-itself is that form of consciousness in which man is always aware of a "lack" or "nothingness" (Sartre, 1966: 617) in him and is always in self-transcendence wherein "our existence from monent to moment is a perpetual flying beyond ourselves, or else a perpetual falling behind our own possibilities: in any case, our being never coincides with itself" (Barret: 118). Due to this, man's existence is personified agony caused by nausea and fallenness. A perfect example of this is the modern man whose life has become meaningless.

Albert Camus (1913-1960) is the proponent of the widely known existentialism of the absurd. The horrors of twentieth century, which he calls "a century of fear," shook him and developed in him an antitheistic existentialist thinker. Throughout his works, Camus expresses a longing for better life and as a positive humanist, he exhorts people to revolt after being baffled by the buffets of the absurd in their life. His slogan is "to create, to transform the humanity of the world into the image of man, to humanize what is inhuman—in short to civilize" (Bree: 3). His revolting hero has to create personal values for himself: "Meaning has to be created, not found, and it has to be created by the individual out of the actual experience of revolt" (Cruikshank: 7).

Camus finds man deprived of grace and justice and wants this revolt to restore man's dignity and honour. In his writings, the rebel protests against the human condition in general. Such rebellion means protest against suffering, death and all sorts of evil. Camus affirms: "Man's solidarity is founded upon rebellion and rebellion can only be justified by his solidarity" (Camus, 1973: 27). Further he explains: "I rebel, therefore I exist" (*Ibid*: 28). In his *The Myth of Sisyphus,* Camus explicates that

"There is but one truly serious philosophical problem, and that is suicide" (Camus, 1975: 39) and "the feeling of estrangement between a man and his life, which sometimes ends in suicide, is the most elementary way of experiencing the absurd" (Camus, 1960: 46). For Camus, Sisyphus, the ancient hero, is the symbol of mankind. He spends his days rolling a rock to the top of a mountain whence the stone would fall back because of its own weight. Camus observes, "No punishment is worse than a task that is useless and without hope" (Camus, 1973: 164) and "the absurd in human being is wedded to life. Life is our rock" (*Ibid*: 267). Suicide, thus, is an act of self-preservation in a way "the man who kills himself in solitude still recognizes a value" (*Ibid*: 15).

Modern Existentialism, though termed by some critics as "the shocking, the sordid, or the obscene" (Greene: 10) and "nearly meaningless" (*Ibid.*), exerted a great impression on some of the non-philosophical writers like Fyodor Dostoevsky (1821-1881), Andre Gide (1869-1951) and Franz Kafka (1883-1924) who dealt with existentialist themes and contributed to the growth of existentialist literature. Other writers who were profoundly affected are Virginia Woolf, Graham Greene, T.S. Eliot, Samuel Beckett, James Joyce, William Golding, William Faulkner and Ernest Hemingway. In Indian English novels, however, the effect of modern existentialism became apparent only after 1950s in the works of Anita Desai and Arun Joshi but it was appropriated and modulated by the ethos of Hindu existential vision. It seems to be a highly rewarding project to explicate Arun Joshi's novels to see how Hindu existential vision can serve as a possible solution to the modern value crisis and materialistic conflicts.

The foregoing discussion demonstrates that Arun Joshi is a significant novelist of post-Independence phase of Indian literature in English. While deeply rooted in Hindu Scriptures, he has also assimilated Western influences in his creative works which centre around the problem of man to find a meaning of life. His protagonists invariably take plunge into challenging predicaments to assert (and redefine as it were) human dignity. The protagonist of his first novel *The Foreigner*, Sindi Oberoi and his odyssey to be taken up in the chapter that follows evidence that Joshi's priority was predominantly human situation and its complexities.

WORKS CITED

Banerjee, Purabi. "A Winner's Secrets," *The Sunday Statesman* (Calcutta), 27 Feb. 1983, 4.

Barret, William. *Irrational Man*. New York: Doubleday and Co., 1962.

Bree, Germaine, (ed). *Camus: A Collection of Critical Essays*. New York: O.U.P., 1968.

Camus, Albert. *The Myth of Sisyphus*. Harmondsworth: Penguin Books, 1975.

——. *The Rebel*. Harmondsworth: Penguin Books, 1973.

Cruickshank, John. *Albert Camus & The Literature of Revolt*. New York: O.U.P., 1960.

Grene, Marjorie. *Introduction To Existentialism*. Chicago: The University of Chicago Press, 1970.

Heidegger, Martin. *An Introduction To Metaphysics* (tr.), R. Nanheim. New York: Doubleday and Co., 1961.

Iyengar, K.R.S. *Indian Writing in English*. New Delhi: Sterling, 1962; rptd., 1996.

Jaspers, Karl. *Man In The Modern Age*. New York: Doubleday and Co., 1956.

Macquarrie, John. *Existentialism*. Harmondsworth: Penguin Books, 1972; rptd. 1986.

Marcel, Gabriel. *The Existential Background To Human Dignity*. New York: Harper and Bros., 1969.

Nietzsche, Friedrich. *The Joyful Wisdom*. (tr.), Thomas Common, London: Macmillan, 1910.

——. *Thus Spake Zarathustra*. (tr.), A. Tille and M.M. Bozman. New York: Dutton, 1933.

Piciucco, Pier Paolo. "An Interview with Arun Joshi," *The Journal of Indian Writing in English*. 25, 1-2(1997), 87-95.

Radhakrishnan, S (ed. & tr.). *The Bhagavadgita*. New Delhi: Harper Collins Publishers, 1993; rptd. 2000.

——. *Eastern Religions and Western Thought*. New Delhi: O.U.P., 1974.

——. (ed. & tr.). *The Principal Upanishads*. New Delhi: Harper Collins Publishers, 1994; rptd. 2000.

Sartre, Jean Paul. *Being and Nothingness: An Essay on Phenomenological Ontology* (tr.). Hazel Barnes. New York: Washington Square Press, 1966.

——. *Existentialism & Humanism* (tr.). Philip Maret as *The Mentor Philosophers*. New York: O.U.P., 1955.

2

REDEMPTION THROUGH ACTION: *THE FOREIGNER*

Arun Joshi's first novel *The Foreigner* (1968) epitomises the main traits of his obsessive preoccupations as a creative artist. Its protagonist, Sindi Oberoi anticipates all his successors in that he shares with them an extremely sensitive and individualistic temperament. As a novelist Joshi has addressed himself to the problem of human dilemmas in all their complexities. More often than not, his protagonists seem to be his mouthpieces advocating implicitly their creator's perception of reality. He candidly admitted to Purabi Banerjee while talking about *The Foreigner*:

> It is largely autobiographical. I am...a somewhat alienated man myself...some parts of *The Foreigner*, my first book, were written when I was a student in America. I gave it up then and completed it later in 1966 (Banerjee: 4).

Later in the same interview he treats this novel as "a study in alienation" (*Ibid*: 4). It is obvious that in Joshi's creative universe the man who suffers and the artist who creates are intricately linked with each other and this lends an unusual authenticity to his novels.

This 'study in alienation' at once recalls the most gripping enigma of human situation in twentieth century. The very title *The Foreigner* reminds one of the epoch making work *The Outsider* by Albert Camus and betrays the essentially serious content of the work. The novel is written from the protagonist-narrator point of view and describes the experiences of the hero, Sindi Oberoi as a student of Mechanical Engineering in the American University in Boston and later as an employee in the firm of Mr. Khemka, a wealthy industrialist in Delhi. After the first chapter which deals with the death of Babu Rao Khemka, the son of Mr. Khemka in a car accident in Boston, the novelist puts the readers to speculate about the emotional impact of Babu's death upon Sindi and Babu's fiance, June and the further events are unfolded with the help of flash-back technique.

Sindi Oberoi, the narrator hero of the novel presents himself as an uprooted young man living in the later half of the twentieth century who wants to arrive at some meaning of his life. He seems a foreigner to the world wherever he goes and at times even becomes a stranger to himself. An Indian by origin, born and brought up in Kenya, Sindi receives his early education in London and goes to study engineering in America. His parents had died in an air crash in his infancy and their only reality for him is "a couple of wrinkled and cracked photographs" (Joshi, 1968: p. 12). This fluidity of his background emphasises his alienation and his being a foreigner from birth. Being orphaned at an early state he finds himself drifting aimlessly on the surface of life without any anchor to cling to. He grows up without family ties and without a country. "My foreignness lay within me" (p. 55), he confesses.

Sindi has vague memories of his parents. When his American beloved June Blyth asks him how long he has been affected by asthma, he answers, "As long as I can remember. They say my mother had it" (p. 32). Thus in Sindi's life, except for a very short time that he spends with his uncle, there is hardly any parental influence. He expresses a peculiar sense of this parental void:

> Anyway I can't really be called a Hindu. My mother was English and my father, I am told, a sceptic. That doesn't seem like a good beginning for a Hindu, does it? (p. 30).

In this way his parentlessness has its manifold implications in the different facets of his life and "he grows up without family ties and without a country" (Naik: 230). He is a child to none. He "is an alien everywhere physically as well as metaphorically" (Mukherjee: 202-203). Being a stranger to the world of filial relationships, he learns some meaning and purpose of life with his uncle. When his uncle's death snaps the last thread of parental love, life becomes a purposeless existence to him. He says:

> Somebody has begotten me without a purpose and so far I had lived without a purpose.... I hadn't felt that when my uncle was living...the thought that he moved about in that small house on the outskirts of Nairobi gave me a feeling of having an anchor. After his death the security was destroyed. Now I suppose I existed only for dying (pp. 55-56).

This loss of personal history, culture and national identity catapults him, as it were into the role of a detached observer or narrator of the whole drama of existence. His is a case of "sociological anomic resulting in ontological insecurity or the psychosis of engulfment" (Prasad: 29). Sindi becomes an anomic man and as a pessimistic narrator tells the story of June, Babu, Shiela, Khemka, Muthu, Karl, Anna, Kathy, Judy etc. Though his own life interferes in the story, he relates his experiences in a stream of consciousness manner. His past experience with the world, the death of his parents and the loneliness in his life makes him totally pessimistic and lost.

While engaged in an amorous sport with June, Sindi marks the sudden fall of a spider from the ceiling, and attributes it to his "exploring his inverted universe" (p. 90). This ordinary and almost negligible incident becomes for him a symbol of man's mysterious position in this universe. According to Sindi, life is shortlived, unreal and inescapably painful. He broods over his loneliness in the ball of International Students Association which is intended to bring foreigners in contact with the Americans:

> Except for the bartender and me there wasn't a soul in the room who wasn't dancing or talking or beating his feet to music. It is remarkable how you can be in a crowded room like that and still feel lonely, like you were sitting in your own tomb (p. 22).

Thus Sindi Oberoi is totally isolated from the whole set-up of society, as a critic perceptively says: "A strange feeling of aloneness and aloofness permeates the entire narrative and provides the necessary texture and structure to the novel" (Bhatnagar: 13-14). Sindi believes that man is just a toy in the hands of time and life is full of agony and pain. In his life, he comes in contact with three persons intimately. His first exposure to relationship is with June Blyth who lives with her mother in Boston. June Blyth is beautiful, sensual, benign, affectionate girl who meets Sindi at a foreign students' party. Being free, frank and generous, she gives of herself abundantly to Sindi as "she thinks it worthwhile to love somebody, make somebody happy..." (p. 92). June loves Sindi deeply but this love is not sincerely reciprocated by Sindi. He, on the other hand, is confused and afraid of human relationships, because they eventually give pain and suffering. He thinks of them as burden upon his self: "I walked down the stairs wishing God has given me greater strength of enduring the burdens of friendship" (p. 18). He believes that he should take lessons from his past and try to remain uninvolved as much as possible. Living in America he is fed up with his life and his routine. He says:

> Each season was the same: working late into night, eating alone in cheap cafeterias, attending weekend cooking sessions at the flat of a countryman. This was the sum total of a foreign student's existence... Fed up with many things. Fed up with the way we pretend to have forgotten the past and yet all the time we are looking for an opportunity to revive it. Fed up with puerile demonstrations of love (p. 25).

Sindi's bright career prospects and enviable academic achievements are of no avail because from all sides, he is overwhelmed by a nagging sense of loneliness and the chaos of his being. He is painfully aware of his miserable past:

> Twenty five years largely wasted in search of wrong things at wrong places. Twenty five years gone in search of peace, and what did I have to show for achievement: a ten stone body that had to be fed four times a day, twenty eight times a week. This was the sum of life time of striving (p. 80).

What oppresses the protagonist most is the realisation that he is a lone person who has failed to see in what way did he belong to the outer world. He fails to see any purpose of his existence. He wants to justify his existence by taking recourse to philosophies when he discusses his problems with the Catholic priest but fails. He says: "I was born a Catholic and I was a great Church-goer until I was fifteen.... One Sunday everything seemed false, the opposite of what it had been. Everybody around me seemed to be play-acting. The priest read his sermons just like my uncle read the markets aloud from the newspaper every morning" (p. 30).

His girl friend June Blyth finds him a queer person because he lacks spontaneity and warmth of a person who enjoys being with others. She tells Sindi:

> There is something strange about you, you know, somewhat distant. I'd guess that when people are with you they don't feel like they are with a human being.... I have a feeling you'd be a foreigner everywhere (p. 29).

In this way Sindi proves himself to be somewhat different from the common run of the people. He spells out his predicament, "My foreignness lay within me and I couldn't leave myself behind wherever I went" (p. 55).

A person who has a balanced temperament enjoys the company of others and forgets himself as well as his ego and is capable of responding spontaneously and productively. He forgets about himself, about his knowledge, about his position and ideas he cherishes. Unfortunately, this is not the case with Sindi. He turns out to be an anomic man. The theory of French sociologist Durkheim and Robert K. Merton on alienation or anomie is expressed by Robert M. MacIver as follows:

> Anomie signifies the state of mind of one who has been pulled up from his moral roots—who has no longer any sense of continuity of folk or sense of obligation. The anomic man has become spiritually sterile, responsive only to himself, responsible to no one (MacIver: 84).

Sindi's case clearly meets this alienated state of life. He has no faith in religion as well at this juncture. When June asks him if he believes in God, Sindi finds himself in a dilemma and shows himself sceptical about the existence of God:

> "She asked me again if I believed in God. I said I didn't know. But I supposed I didn't" (p. 30).

He has a purely detached business-like attitude towards life and people. Sitting expressionless, he watches the world go by. Thus Sindi is a psychic case. He is totally unaware of the happiness provided by emotional bonds. Earlier in England he had amorous relationships with Anna and Kathy but all his relationships "fizzled out like an ill packed cracker" (p. 121) because be couldn't pay the price of being loved. Sindi's past experience has given him painful lessons: "Even after several years, somewhere in the labyrinth of my consciousness the wound still bled. I felt sad and perhaps showed it" (p. 61).

To get rid of his past he tries hard to involve himself in some work but is far from getting it. When he visits the house of June Blyth in Boston, June tries to involve him in a conversation with a view to knowing more and more about him. But it makes him uneasy. He feels embarrassed by her personal talk and changes the subject to save himself from the discomfort of talking about himself. He all along desires to physically possess her but wildly struggles to remain uninvolved. In fact, he entertains a deep sense of insecurity, unreality and impermanence about things. In one of his conversations with his beloved June Blyth, he says:

> ...I have loved people as much as I love myself. It isn't much but that is not my fault. And then to be in love in your sense requires one to take things seriously, assume that there is a permanence about things. Nothing ever seems real to me, leave alone permanent. Nothing seems to be very important (p. 92).

These words betray his depressing attitude towards life. First of all Sindi doesn't love himself sufficiently well to love others. He cannot love himself because he suffers from a self-defeating sense of insecurity. His defences not only disallow him to love others but also be loved by others as he himself confesses: "I was not the kind of man one could love; I had learnt that long ago" (p. 34). Sindi had never learnt to take things seriously. His casuality therefore forces him to deny the reality and permanence of things and life. This attitude develops in him a fear of involvement, which can be observed from his ruminations:

> "I don't want to get involved," I repeated to myself. Everywhere I turned I saw involvement (pp. 62-63).

At the same time he indulges himself with Anna and is seduced by her, who is a middle-aged woman of "thirty five with dark hair and finely chiselled features" (p. 176). She is "a minor artist who had separated from her husband" (p. 142). He has a love affair with her and comes to know after some time that "Anna was not yearning for me or anybody, but for her lost youth" (p. 143). Though attracted by her sadness Sindi fails to continue with her for more than six months: "We carried on like this for six months, I think she loved me intensely and unselfishly, I enjoyed making love to her and her sadness attracted me, but engrossed as I was with my own self I couldn't return her love" (p. 143). Later on he gets involved with Kathy and enjoys sex with her but she also leaves him because she is a married woman and thinks that "marriage was sacred and had to be maintained at all costs" (p. 144). After her return to her husband he comes to experience the same with Judy and Christine but these transitory pleasures leave him unsatisfied and agonised. He comes to the conclusion that "marriage was more often a lust for possession than anything else. People got married just as they bought new cars. And then they gobbled each other up" (p. 60).

Sindi goes on talking and behaving disinterestedly with June and June's sincere efforts to involve Sindi in a loving union fail due to his ego which forces him to practise detachment. Though Sindi continues his passionate affair with June for quite a long time, he tries not to get attached to her for "One should be able to love without wanting to possess.... One should be able to detach oneself from the object of one's love" (p. 60). Time and again June requests him to get married to her: "Let's get married, Sindi. For God's sake, let's get married" (p. 107). He seems to quibble with her in order to underscore the importance of his detachment in love:

> Absence of love does not mean hatred. Hatred is just another form of love. There is another way of loving. You can love without attachment, without desire. You can love without attachment to the objects of your love. You can love without fooling yourself that the things which you love are indispensable either to you or to the world. Love is real only when you know that what you love must one day die (p. 145).

In this way Sindi stubbornly refuses to succumb to June's love and to loosen his grip on his creed of detachment and non-involvement. He believes that man is just a toy in the hands of time having nothing to do but wait till time decides the future. Sindi subscribes to the view of Arun who is also an Indian student abroad: "Random events happen around you forcing you to make decisions propelling you on through life. It is only your vanity that makes us imagine that we are leading our own destiny" (p. 68). Sindi further adds to this that to believe that man acts as a free agent is mere an illusion and nothing else:

> But you are never free, Karl. How can anybody take away your freedom when you never had it in the first place? All freedom is illusion. You had no choice in your birth nor do you even choose your death. And in between is a vast expanse of lawless sands that pile up where the wind blows (pp. 67-68).

With such a peculiar cast of mind, he is drawn towards a series of women though it is only with June that he is brought face to face with his hypocrisy, cowardice, vanity and stupidity. He enjoys making love to her as it feeds his vanity to know that there is someone who finds him worthy of love. June, on the other hand loves Sindi not to leave him alone as she "was one of those persons who have the capacity to forget themselves in somebody's trouble" (p. 97). Being a source of such an enduring love, June fails to understand the efficacy of Sindi's detachment. She wants to marry him, but he is least inclined to marriage, since it means "possessing" and "being possessed" and says: "It is not that all marriages are painful...it is one big illusion that has been pounded into them by society. For a while they go around bloated with their own pride imagining things which just are not there. And then gradually the whole thing crumbles and they begin to kill each other bit by bit" (p. 91). He attempts to explain further:

> Marriage wouldn't help, June. We are alone, both you and I. That is the problem. And our aloneness must be resolved from within. You can't send two persons through a ceremony and expect that their aloneness will disappear... (p. 107).

Although he loves her with a strange fierceness he does not accede to her proposal of marriage. He believes that marriage is a big illusion and "Death wipes out everything for most of us anyway. All that is left is a big mocking zero" (p. 92). To him, "Good things and bad things appear to be the same in the long run of existence" (p. 93). Thus a realisation of the absurdity of human situation can be seen in his self and his refusal to marry June only heightens it. Defining the meaning of the term 'absurd' Eugene Ionesco observes:

> Absurd is that which is devoid of purpose...cut off from his religious, metaphysical and transcendental roots, man is lost; all his actions become senseless, absurd, useless (Ionesco: 56).

Sindi thus becomes a typical Sartrean hero who expresses his metaphysical anguish at the meaninglessness of the human condition and reminds us of Roquentin, Sartre's hero of *Nausea* who reflects on the absurdity of existence:

> We were a heap of existents inconvenienced, embarrassed by ourselves, we hadn't the slightest reason for being there, any of us, each existent, embarrassed, vaguely ill at ease, felt superfluous in relation to others (Sartre: 184).

The other man of importance with whom Sindi involves himself is Babu Rao Khemka whom he meets while working for his doctoral degree in Boston. Babu is an oversheltered son of a Delhi tycoon and sees America as a paradise for free sexes and argues with Sindi, "What is the good of coming to America if one is not to play around with girls?" (p. 20) exhibiting the image of an indefatiguable half-baked Indian casanova abroad. He wants to make American friends and not to mix with Indians all the time. Sindi's association with Babu gives the former a clear picture of an educated and rich Indian family. Babu's father Mr. Khemka has brought his son up with all the care which is expected of him. He tells Sindi, "I had brought him up with all the care that a father can give to a child.... Even as a child, I had myself taught him what was right and what was wrong" (p. 119).

On account of this over protectiveness, Babu has innocence and simplicity but not the toughness of experience as one may expect of him and a critic rightly observes: "Even since his childhood, he has been fed up on the hygienic diet of morals, even so he does not apply himself to his pursuit with the seriousness that is expected of him" (Jha: 173). Sindi finds Babu as only "a kid," an innocent little rich father's boy and makes a general observation on all such Indian boys: "That was how they all began when they came. They wanted to play around. They forgot that one couldn't play around without playing with oneself and that could be fatal" (p. 21).

If Sindi is a shirker, Babu is too much anchored to his parents. They possess Babu so much that they deprive him of his free will, hampering his capacity to make resolutions. Even as Babu continues his studies at Boston, he is always apprehensive of his father's admonitions. In the meanwhile he is attracted to June; when she comes to know about Babu's situation, she observes:

> This father of his seems to be an awful bully. I am sure things would be much simpler if he (father) were not always there in the background, sending those long sermons and telling him what's wrong with him and how he should carry himself (p. 105).

Babu is always filled with awe at the thought of his failure at the examination and the frustration of his father's expectations. Sindi is no different from Babu. While Babu is incapable of making resolutions Sindi does not make them "because the pain of breaking them was too unbearable" (p. 156). One can not take decisions, the other would not for fear of decisions. One is undercontrolled, the other over-controlled. Both are basically cowards either haunted by the presence of parents or by the depressive memories of their parents.

After Sindi's refusal to marry June, it is perhaps natural that June and Babu should meet more often and avoid Sindi. After some days Sindi rings June and requests her to dine with him. She declines the invitation: "I'm sorry, Sindi, I will not be able to see you anywhere, I mean not as I used to, Babu and I are getting married soon" (p. 111). When he puts down the receiver, he presses his face hard against the metal of the telephone and cries. By this time all his carefully cultivated detachment has vanished and Sindi is utterly miserable: "The edge of pain was so intense that it left me completely numb" (p. 123).

Sindi remains in a state of coma for some time as he is totally broken after receiving this shock. Gradually his coma lessens, as he is aided by his work at the college. At this point he behaves like a typical lover. It is strange that though Sindi is not willing to marry June, he is deeply depressed and agonised when she is separated from him. Sindi is not like a man immune to all emotions as he thinks he is. Even now and then he finds himself in places where he had been with her. "Here is where we met, here I bought a book, there she wanted me to kiss her, and my heart would sink with the burden of my memories and I couldn't help whispering to myself, My darling! Oh, my darling!" It can be very well observed that these are not the words of "one who should be able to detach oneself from the object of one's love" (p. 60).

Thus Sindi is totally confused regarding what kind of dogma or rules to adopt and what kind of life to lead. He just keeps on jumping from one to another set of rules and finds nothing. Sometimes he talks about the inevitability of things and sometimes about detachment. He talks of detachment and gets involved everywhere. His belief that the whole world is an illusion (*maya*) haunts him. Sindi accepts his confusion in these words: "I had wanted detachment but I didn't know what kind of resolutions were necessary to achieve it" (p. 66).

The other episode makes Sindi's failure at the practical side of life more clear. Babu, who is now June's lover is conscious of the attitude of his father towards love and marriage. Further, when June asks Babu to marry her, he expresses his helplessness: "He sent me here and I promised him I'll never marry in America" (p. 100). Inspite of all this, Babu and June are betrothed and this comes as a blow to Sindi. He is totally helpless because he has himself allowed this to happen. He has had many relationships, but whenever there is a question of marriage, he has tried to be excused on the pretext of remaining detached. Though he voices his interest in finding a "meaning of life" and his effort "to do something meaningful" (p. 14), his escapist tendency is the result of his belief in the impermanence of things. As he tells June "Nothing seems real to me, leave alone permanent. Nothing seems to be important" (p. 92) his entire life is a quest for the permanence in life. In his eagerness to find out this, Sindi lives in a strange world of intense pleasure and pain. But he fails to make satisfactory progress and his twenty five years are "largely wasted in search of wrong things in wrong places" (p. 80).

Sindi's sufferings are manifestations of a spiritual crisis which all sensitive and introvert people have to face in life. He wants peace, a capacity to love and the courage to live without desire and attachment. His main intention is "to conquer pain" and death which "wipes out everything" leaving only "a big mocking zero" (p. 92). His various experiences in life, however leave him with unanswered questions "like swollen carcasses strewn on river banks after a flood" (p. 92). He is keen on knowing his purpose in life whose knowledge is essential before he can make earnest efforts to fulfil it. He feels always being pushed "on the giant wheel, going round and round, waiting for the fall" (p. 75).

The "pathlessness" of the road to New York reminds Sindi of his own pathlessness. He remembers the lines from a popular song which runs:

> Who knows, who knows
> Where the road will lead?
> Only a fool can say (p. 152).

He considers his life as a labyrinth and becomes conscious of life's vagueness:

> Taller than the tallest tree,
> Deeper than the deep blue sea,
> That's how it's going to be,
> All the way (p. 152).

Fully convinced of the meaninglessness of the world, he even contemplates suicide. He does not fit in the world and his way of life seems confused and explains his state as: "cynical and exhausted, grown old before his time, weary with my own loneliness" (p. 131). It is due to this fact that all his decisions and resolutions are initiated by his cynical temper. Sindi does not know that a person who escapes from his duties has nothing in store but pain. Still he cherishes the hope that June may return to him. So when June makes advance to Sindi one night in his apartment, he yields to her. Later June drives to Babu's flat where both of them quarrel and she admits to Babu that she has been sleeping with Sindi. Babu, due to his Indian mental make-up fails to accept the American standards of conduct between the betrothed lovers. He in his fit of temper drives off his car blindly and is killed in the car accident. Both June and Sindi realize that Babu has committed suicide. Babu has been sent out of his college as he had failed in all his exams. He had been disowned by his father for intending to marry June. And to top it all comes June's confession of her relations with Sindi which ultimately prods him to put an end to life.

On his part Sindi feels guilty of having driven a man to death:

> ...it suddenly struck me that something had been knocked out of me. I just was not the same person anymore...I felt as if there was nothing left that I could depend upon.... I felt like a desert or like a vast field of naked oats in winter time. I felt more alone and naked in the world than I had ever felt before (p. 149).

At this point his realisation about his mistaken detachment and involvement starts. He is shocked to find out that he has made himself an accomplice in the murder of an innocent man like Babu. June is no exception to all this. He realizes:

> All along I had acted out of lust and greed and selfishness, and they had applauded my wisdom. When I had sought only detachment I had driven a man to his death. It all seemed very logical now that it happened (p. 8).

When he looks at June when she walks through the revolving doors he observes: "She carried death with her. She had been an accomplice in a murder and she didn't even know it. But ignorance of sin...is no excuse" (p. 9). Out of his despair, he feels that he cannot stay any longer in America and decides to leave for India, but the worse is yet to follow. As he is waiting for the necessary Visa papers in New York, he receives a letter from June telling him that she is carrying Babu's child in her womb. She further requests him to come over to Boston. He finds himself in a dilemma as he cannot leave New York for the next few days. And when he visits June's house, he finds it locked. He is told by her neighbour that June had died after an abortion and that her mother had gone away from the house. The death of June leaves Sindi desperate and he is left musing on his so called creed of non-involvement:

> My parents, my uncle, my lovers, Babu and June, their parents, and finally myself, one by one all were called by the invisible judges and asked to give their evidence (p. 165).

Sindi remembers all that has happened in past and voices man's helplessness in this absurd world. The past comes as a flashback:

> My falling in love with June because she was what I was not; her leaving me for Babu for a dream; because I had lost the capacity to dream; and now finally the end of her dream. And what could I, who had so little control over his own destiny and actions, do to stem the tide whose course was set long ago? (p. 139).

He thinks of himself like a plaything which is tossed here and there and this goads him to observe his past life in retrospection again:

> I joined London University, but very soon I got tired of the classroom lectures. I didn't have any trouble with my

> courses and I passed the exams creditably enough when they came, but the question that bothered me was very different. I wanted to know the meaning of my life. All my classrooms didn't tell me a thing about it. Ultimately, I decided that I needed experience other than studying... (p. 142), (emphases added).

In wanting "to know the meaning of my life", Sindi subjects himself to all sorts of varied experiences only to infer at the end that suffering is inescapable. The death of Babu and June shatters him completely:

> All that I had thought was pleasurable had ended in pain, and after all this I was as far from finding the purpose of my life as I had been to start with. It all puzzled me. And I spent a whole year wandering through the maze of my existence looking for answer. It was not until the next summer that the answer came, not wholly but in a good enough measure, good enough to start with (p. 144).

Thus the novel emphasises through the travails of Sindi the mysterious and incalculable nature of life. The events of life are uncontrollable and one cannot help getting involved inevitably. Sindi aptly says: "One does not choose one's involvement" (p. 41). A deep sense of affliction scourges him and he feels as if there is nothing left for him to depend upon. He is seized with a sense of guilt as he says:

> I had presumed that I could extricate her from the web of her own actions; that I could make her happy by simply standing still and letting her use me whichever way she wished. Nothing could have been farther from the idea of detachment. That was a fatal presumption (p. 165).

June's tragic death acts as a tragic peripeteia. It brings a sudden realization in Sindi and he realises: "Detachment at that time had meant inaction. Now I had begun to see the fallacy in it. Detachment consisted of right action and not escape from it" (p. 162). Though this revelation has come to him somewhat late but the lesson he has got from all this is of utmost significance. He identifies his situation precisely:

> An uprooted young man living in the later half of twentieth century who has become detached from everything except himself. Where Kathy and Anna had taught me to be detached from others. June's death finally broke my attachment to myself. It was here that my hope lay (p. 164).

To put it still more clearly he employs a metaphor: "...I felt as if some indefatigable surgeon was cleaning up my soul with the sharp edge of his scapel" (p. 165). A therapeutic process has set in and it might enable him derive some meaning in an otherwise futile existence.

Depending as much on luck as on careful planning Sindi happens to come to India, the land of his ancestors. He goes to meet Babu's father and sister in Delhi. Babu's father, Mr. Khemka and his sister, Shiela put to him all sorts of questions about Babu's stay in States including his relationship with June who in their perception caused Babu's death. Sindi's attempts at convincing them of reality prove of no avail. In the meanwhile he is invited to work as Mr. Khemka's personal assistant to help him in all his activities and he accepts the offer. After working with them for sometime Sindi feels disenchanted by the mode of life and set of values which Khemka and his friends follow and treats this atmosphere as a more vile version of life which he had already experienced in America. Their shameless and immoral attempts to obtain material possessions leaves him deeply demoralised. He gives vent to his feelings to Shiela:

> Your father loved him like a factory. Babu was a pawn in your father's hand with no will or life of his own. That's why he couldn't bear the thought of Babu marrying June. It did not fit in his plans. He wanted to marry Babu to a fat Marwari girl whose dowry might bring him half a dozen new factories (p. 51).

Despite being labelled as Indian Sindi finds himself uncomfortable:

> I was considered quite a misfit. My foreign background stood against me. Nobody hated me. I was too insignificant for that sort of thing. But I suspect they considered me a

> little too casual even though some of them envied me a bit for my light-heartedness (p. 15).

The social parties arranged frequently at Mr. Khemka's house are all a bit of a hoax for Sindi who regards this scenario as just a change of theatre from America. When he notices the bronze figure of the dancing Shiva in the dining room of the Khemkas, he is reminded of the dance of the divine dancer:

> I was stuck by the intense beauty of the divine dancer. America, India, Egypt, all mingled behind him in aeons of increasing rhythm. The dance went on unheeding, and yet comprehending all. What did it matter if Babu was dead, and I living merely to keep up appearances (p. 14).

The image of dancing Shiva speaks of the oriental philosophical influence on Arun Joshi. Shiva is both 'Rudra' (destructive power) and 'Shiva' (benign force) and Sindi is the quester who has been undergoing a complete overhauling. The birth of a new man is taking place within him and as a progression of this metamorphosis Sindi intuitively realises the operation of the law of *karma* because he finds that the seemingly separate experiences of life are related to form the pattern of his life. His faith in the law of *karma* is affirmed in his thought that "we think we leave our actions behind but the past is never dead. Time has a way of exacting its toll and the more you try to hold, the heavier the toll is" (p. 181). This realisation induces him to measure his past and he says:

> It seemed that I had never done anything except wait on that narrow bed. The room dissolved in the heat and I was sitting in the middle of a desert waiting for a prophet (p. 171).

Now onwards he behaves in a more confident way with Mr. Khemka and Shiela. He goes to the extent of vehemently condemning Mr. Khemka:

> It is you who have swindled those miserable wretches in rags who push carts on your streets and die at twenty five. It is you who have been telling lies and fabricating documents just so that you could air-condition this

> ostentatious house and throw gigantic parties for the horde of jackals who masquerade as your friends (p. 180).

Sindi feels utterly disgusted at the modus operandi of Mr. Khemka and his tribe who exploit needy people like Jain and Muthu so that their empire could grow. When after an income tax raid, Khemka tries to influence Sindi with money to accept the blame upon himself and save Mr. Khemka from the disgrace of arrest and imprisonment, Sindi feels so much shocked that he decides to move away from Khemka's world. There are rumours of Khemka's firm being bought over by some other greedy shark. Muthu requests him to take over the office so that the poor workers of the factory are not ousted from job. The heroic struggle of Muthu to provide food to his own family and the family of his brother, who is unemployed, reveals to Sindi the real meaning of life which one finds in developing sympathetic understanding with other persons and responding to them warmly. That afternoon, when the sky is clear, Sindi goes to meet Muthu. The clear sky symbolises the light of knowledge that will dawn upon Sindi. Muthu, an almost illiterate labourer, teaches Sindi Oberoi, a Ph.D. in Mechanical Engineering from U.S.A. the sharp distinction between detachment and involvement—"Sometimes detachment lies in actually getting involved" (p. 188).

Muthu and his problems bring about a major change in Sindi's attitude towards life. Muthu is human suffering personified for him with a daughter in her frock much "dirty and too large" for her and with a wife suffering from tuberculosis that rather "gets bad in that weather" of rains. Gradually he develops empathy even for other labourers working for Mr. Khemka:

> It was a sad sight. The workers' clothes were falling off in rags and sweat poured off their backs as if they had just had a shower.... These are my people, I thought. And yet I moved among them as if I were a stranger (p. 166).

It is "the accumulated despair of their weary lives" (p. 189) that makes Sindi take over the management of the imprisoned Mr. Khemka's business, as utterly challenging situation:

> I felt as if I had been dropped on a sinking ship and charged with the impossible task of taking it ashore (p. 189).

All of a sudden Sindi cancels his visit to Bombay to take up a new assignment and unpacks his things and puts them "back as neatly possible in their old places" (p. 189) and reviews his past in these words:

> Before I went to sleep that night I took a general stock of myself. In many ways the past had been a waste, but it had not been without its lessons. I had started adult life as a confused adolescent, engrossed with myself, searching for wisdom and the peace that comes with it. The journey had been long and still was not over (p. 185).

Given his past track record, it is a sea change in him as it shows his stubbornness to meet life on his terms. He plunges himself into the battle of survival which the workers of the factory could not have won without his help, co-operation and guidance. Deeply aware of this new orientation in his way of life which leads him to affirmation, he gives a new orientation to his name too and instead of 'Surendra' or 'Surinder' he calls himself 'Surrender Oberoi' (p. 191). Thus Sindi becomes a typical existential hero, the haunted anguished creature of Sartre who is absolutely alone and free, creating himself a personal way of life out of the void of nothingness all round him. He finds relief from his agony when he comes to India and is satisfied with his involvement in right action. India makes him shift the attachment from the self to the world. The sense of guilt which has oppressed him since Babu committed suicide is erased by this realisation that Babu's father is a cheat. The journey from the West to East symbolises Sindi's spiritual quest. Sindi's long and circuitous journey helps him recognise the meaning and purpose of life. Muthu for him becomes the most appropriate example of the ideal man—the man of steady wisdom. In *The Bhagavadgita*, the Blessed Lord says:

> *tasmad asaktah satatam*
> *karyam karma samachara*

> *asakto hy acaran karma*
> *param apnoti purusah*
>
> Therefore, without attachment, perform always the work that has to be done, for man attains to the highest by doing work without attachment (Radhakrishnan, 1993: 138).

Through the character and ordeals of Sindi, Arun Joshi demonstrates that non-attachment can be acquired in stages only. The juncture which Sindi reaches is an important intermediary stage of the individual's attachment with the world combined with his non-attachment with himself. The novel portrays the progress of a Sartrean protagonist attached only with his own self towards a realisation of humanity and responsibility which brings him very close to the concept of '*karmayoga*' of *The Bhagavadgita* as the Lord puts it:

> *Karmany eva dhikaras te*
> *ma phalesu kadachana*
> *ma karmaphalhetur bhur*
> *ma te sango stu akarmani*
>
> (To action alone hast thou a right and never at all to its fruits; let not the fruits of action be thy motive; neither let there be in thee any attachment to inaction) (*Ibid*: 119).

The Foreigner has evoked varied response from scholars and critics. While to Verghese, the novel advocates "the idea of non-attachment as a solution to the problem of loneliness and rootlessness" (Verghese: 124). Jain regards the final decision on Sindi's part as an act of "disinterested involvement" (Jain: 54). Another critic says that "Twice removed from his country of birth, therefore an alien everywhere, Sindi wished to achieve equipose through non-attachment in vain" (Singh: 176). In the light of such comments, invariably centered on Sindi's behaviour though they have their own validity, it is possible to read the novel from still another perspective. At a deeper level, *The Foreigner* can be viewed as an attempt to plumb man's perennial dilemmas. In the novel, Sindi's essential responses are projected in two situations: his relationships with June Blyth in Boston, and his contact with the Khemkas in Delhi. To understand Sindi it is essential that one analyses his responses to the institution of marriage and to the world of commercial deals. After much suffering experienced in relationships with Anna and Cathy, he discovers that marriage is no answer to the basic questions that disturb his mind. His psychosomatic asthma can at best be sympathetically observed by June but cannot be cured by her. In a starkly realistic mood he questions the value of marriage as a safety valve. Explaining this to June he says: "You can't send two persons through a ceremony and expect that their aloneness will disappear" (p. 107). It is Sindi's mature realisation that prevents him from viewing life as a perpetual carnival and leads him to believe that ultimately it is limbo that squarely stares one in the face. He remarks, "Death wipes out every thing for most of us anyway. All that is left is a big mocking zero" (p. 92) which is an obvious Indian standpoint of observing things.

Sindi is equally candid in criticising the rapid advancement of technology: "America is a place for well-fed automations rushing about in automatic cars. I'd go mad if I had to do that" (p. 78). However, he is not blind to the life-sustaining signals from the bountiful flora in America:

> Whatever griefs you may have had in your private universe, spring in America ruthlessly extracted its toll of gaity (p. 128).

It is this openness of Sindi's self that the Khemkas fail to appreciate. Mr. Khemka is shocked by Sindi's indifference towards the commercial prospects and when he expresses his disappointment, Sindi replies without mincing words:

> I am not strange. I am perhaps different from you and your world. My set of experiences has taught me a reality that is different from yours (p. 117).

He is still more explicit further:

> You had a clear-cut system of morality, a caste system that laid down all you had to do. You had a God; you had roots in the soil you lived upon. Look at me. I have no roots. I have no system of morality.... You ask me why I am not

> ambitious; well, I have no reason to be. Come [sic] of it. I don't even have a reason to live! (p. 118).

He is unsparing even to Mr.Khemka's daughter Sheila: "Life is not a business account, losses of which can be written off against the gains. Once your soul goes bankrupt, no amount of plundering can enrich it again" (p. 122). Such scathing comments amply evidence that Sindi is not ready to lose his soul as do the Khemkas in the frenzied pursuit of affluence. Sindi's long journey—Kenya-London-Boston-Delhi—is structured round his central concern for the affirmation of life and his employment with the Khemkas turns out to be an infinitely rewarding experience.

Though Sindi involves himself in an earnest quest for life-sustaining values, he is not able to overcome the miseries of past completely. He also knows that one is ought to be held responsible for one's action, an intuitive realisation of the operation of the Law of *Karma.* Once Sindi realises that "there is a chance to redeem the past" he detaches himself from his ego, transcends his self-absorption and wrecklessly involves himself in lives, other than his own. The close of the novel testifies to such an assumption as reflected in his last meeting with Shiela. When she gets up and is on the point of leaving his office, Sindi requests her to stay on for some time: "If you can wait ten minutes, I will come with you... May be we could have tea at Wengers" (p. 191). This invitation coming as it does from a man who has very bitter memories of female relationship, is a significant pointer to the change in Sindi's behaviour. His invitation to her for a cup of tea at Wengers may not be treated as an act of mere formality. That Sindi and Shiela has been at loggerheads in respect of their attitudes of material concerns, among many other things. Such courtesy speaks of Sindi's involvement with the human situation. No wonder Shiela reciprocates at the restaurant, "Shall we have some tea?", the concluding line of the novel. That Arun Joshi should choose to wind up his first creative work with employing the pronoun 'we' in the last line demonstrates that the alienation howsoever dominant as a theme it might appear in the novel has been ultimately overcome. With the coming closer of the two major characters, the affirmative message of the novel is brought home to the reader quite eloquently.

The foregoing analysis demonstrates that Arun Joshi makes use of existentialism, *Vedanta*, the philosophy of *karma* and Lord Krishna's concepts of 'detachment' and 'involvement' in *The Foreigner*. It is to the credit of the novelist that the induction of these philosophical ideas does not mar the aesthetics of the work. Joshi suggests that there is misery and strife in this world caused by misconceptions of certain ideas and that one can carve one's way out of this impasse through a sensible approach to problems. While apparently deriving from the existentialists and the absurdists, his understanding of human situation has a uniqueness and novelty of its own.

Arun Joshi begins the novel with a story interest. It opens in a morgue where Sindi Oberoi has to identify his dead friend Babu Rao Khemka:

> They uncovered his face and I turned in spite of myself.... A dark bottomless hole gaped in the place of the right eye. The sensual upper lip was gone, leaving behind a horrible grin that showed no sign of ending (p. 7).

The story is told in a style of flashback narrative with a clever ordering of past events. Further the novelist mixes together the past and present, the world of imagination as well as reality to maximise the suspense. The cause of Babu's death is not known to the reader until he finishes the two-third of the novel. In the manner of detective story the novelist keeps the readers engaged in speculation. The death of Babu Rao Khemka, the finding of the photograph of June from his wallet, the identification of the dead body by Sindi Oberoi and Shiela's handing over a "frayed envelope" which contains Babu's letters evoke the mystery of a suspense story. At the very outset when he makes his readers inquisitive, Joshi goes to deal with Sindi's background and his relationships mixing together the past and the present. The chronology of events is maintained though the past intrudes by the questions asked by Shiela who is anxious about the death of her brother Babu.

The point of view in the novel is that of autobiography because the narrator-protagonist begins the novel as an 'I' character. Such type of narration is necessary because the novelist deals at length about the hero's psychical contact with society and his psychological developments which enable him to solve his problems. Sindi always remains "detached" to the events of life but towards the end he finds himself involved in the lives of other people. This type of first person narrative enables Arun Joshi to keep his character neutral who can enjoy his own identity from other men and women in the novel as well as from the author himself. Though the novelist remains detached, he quite efficiently surveys both the East and the West in an objective manner. He has chosen Sindi Oberoi, a Kenyan born Indian as the hero of the novel. He is a "foreigner" both for the East and the West. In this way Joshi succeeds in keeping him aloof as well as near these cultures because his mother was a British and his father a Kenyan-Indian. It is this mixed parentage that helps him to look from the human point of view. He does not represent a confrontation between two set of values as we see in the works of cross-culturally preoccupied novelists like Jhabvala and Markandaya. The 'foreigners' in his novels are not very important characters and their contribution lies in their own individual reactions and responses and not in any kind of representation of a set of values.

The subplot of Khemka, his daughter Shiela and Sindi is inextricably woven into the texture of the main plot of Sindi, June and Babu. Mr. Khemka is a pompous businessman who has sent his son to America so that he can talk to his friends about his widely-travelled son. To Mr. Khemka and his daughter Shiela, June is a foreigner who cannot be married to Babu as she does not know the language, the customs, the traditions and the religion of India. Sindi laughs at this and says: "Foreigners don't fit in our homes because we don't want them to fit in" (p. 52). He also mocks at the sex-centred morality of India when Shiela accuses June of not being virtuous on the grounds that she is not a virgin: "So you think one of these Marwari girls is really superior merely because of a silly membrane between her legs?" (p. 52). Mr. Khemka is also a contrast to Sindi in many ways. While Sindi is never sure of himself, Khemka is always sure of himself. He is sure that the poor people are always envious of those who have money. He thinks nothing wrong in making money and only clever people can do so. To him money is the only reality upon this earth. It is for this that Sindi becomes reluctant to pay for the sins of Mr. Khemka. In the last he decides to hold the reins of Khemka's business due to sympathy for the poor employees who face their removal from service. The cynical Sindi changes into a purposeful man. It is here that he "belongs." At this juncture Sindi's problem is the problem of existence, seeking fulfilment in terms of human relationships.

Alienation though suggested from the person of Sindi Oberoi is not real. It is mainly the outcome of such a narrative technique in which Sindi himself as the narrator seems alienated. The use of an outsider's point of view runs side by side to the view of life that Joshi is intended to present. He satirises Indian economic disparity and moral code as well through his characters. Except June and Shiela, all the other characters are mere satirical sketches. Babu's portrait is badly exposed to ridicule. His inexperience is exposed blatantly. He is a typical Indian student abroad; Mr. Khemka, an Indian businessman; Mrs. Blyth an American snob. Babu's innocence leads him to death. Lacking the fighting spirit and unable to face the stark realities of life, he commits suicide. Mr. Khemka is corrupt so he is detained behind the bars. Sindi stands for fortitude against the onslaughts of circumstances. As opposed to them, June is one who has the capacity to forget themselves in somebody's trouble. This is what she does to both the Indian students in America. She wants to be of use to others. She likes people from other countries, especially people from Asia.

Indian English novelists have used myths as structural parallels but Arun Joshi's fiction only sparsely suggests some mythical patterns by viewing certain aspects of situation and character. Sindi resembles Karna, the great character in *The Mahabharata* because both face a crisis of identity. In Karna's case the problem of belonging is brought out by fate and he wants social recognition. In Sindi's case he doesn't have that crisis because the societies are mostly friendly to him. Further Karna, the man of action is in no way comparable to Sindi who is worried about his detachment. There is no earnest attempt on the part of Karna to win Draupadi at the *swayamvara* where he was present but not as a suitor. Sindi, on the other hand, does not want to be involved and possess June but he is jealous of her going to Babu's hands. Sindi can be no match to the mythological hero known for his valour and integrity.

Sindi Oberoi's life can be viewed as a *yatra,* a pilgrimage from meaninglessness to affirmation through knowledge. Sindi after undergoing a long conflict between the saint and the lusty beast in him, reaches a solution to his problem. The first part of the novel is set in the West. The hero of the novel Sindi starts his pursuit to reach beyond the veil which covers reality. This is the only problem he wants his Professor to explain to him. He feels depressed about his education which has denied him right kind of experience and subjects himself to a menial job in the night club in Soho: "I didn't work to earn money. My mind was full of thoughts and I wanted a different kind of experience to sort my ideas out" (p. 167). The journey which a pilgrim undertakes is a testing ground for his commitment and tenacity. Almost all the incidents in the novel like academic success, love and friendship, suicide, death and the downfall of Khemka's empire are touchstones to test his moral principles and wisdom. In this ordeal he behaves like Meursault of *L'Etranger,* and remains unambitious and detached but with a difference. He, in fact, cultivates detachment as a virtue. Mearsault remains the outsider, detached and indifferent to whatever happens to him, the illness and death of his mother, his imprisonment and even the sentence of death awarded to him. Sindi, on the other hand, is humbler enough to learn from the problems of life.

The events of life, however, are uncontrollable and one gets easily trapped in them. The deaths of his friend Babu and his sweetheart June completely drain out his confidence. He comes to realise that involvement without undue attachment is a key to affirmation. In this way Babu and June though dead prompt Sindi to analyse the validity of his detachment and the necessity of love and involvement. This journey from the West to the East helps him to achieve affirmation. "Having become a 'karmayogi' he finds his equanimity and salvation" (Mathur, Rai: 107) in the land of his ancestors. To quote Hari Mohan Prasad, "From Boston to Delhi has been a journey from alienation to arrival, from selfishness to sacrifice, from an anomic responsible to himself to a member of mankind, from being to becoming" (Prasad, 43). Sindi comes to terms with his "foreignness" and feels that there are useful tasks to be done in the future even if the future is as meaningless as the past.

The title of the novel *The Foreigner* itself gains a symbolic importance in the larger context of human existence. It portrays the protagonist's sense of metaphysical anguish at the meaninglessness of his life. The unreality and transitoriness associated with the word 'Foreign' permeates the whole structure of the novel. From this view, *The Foreigner* has a remarkable degree of maturity suited to its theme. The awareness of man's worthless life that breeds consequential anxiety is the keynote of Joshi's vision of the plight of modern man. While Sindi Oberoi eventually perceives release from the anxieties of life through *karmayoga*, the principle of action without attachment, the protagonist of *The Strange Case of Billy Biswas* explores yet another alternative to human position to be taken up in the next chapter.

WORKS CITED

Bannerjee, Purabi. "A Winner's Scerets," *The Sunday Statesman* (Calcutta), 27 Feb. 1983, 4.

Bhatnagar, O.P. "Arun Joshi's *The Foreigner*, A Critique of East and West," *Journal of Indian Writing in English*, 1, 3 (1973), 13-17.

Ionesco, Eugene. "Dans Les armes de la ville," *Cahiers de la Compagnie Madeleine Renand* (tr.), Jean Louis Barrault. Paris, 20 Oct (1957).

Jain, Jasbir. "Foreigners and Strangers: Arun Joshi's Heroes," *Journal of Indian Writing in English*, 5, 1 (1977), 52-57.

Jha, Mohan. "*The Foreigner*, A Study in Innocence and Experience," R.K. Dhawan (ed.), *The Fictional World of Arun Joshi*. New Delhi: Classical Publishing Company, 1986.

Joshi, Arun. *The Foreigner*. Delhi: Hind Pocket, 1968; rptd. Orient Paperbacks, 1993. All citations refer to this edition followed by paginations.

Koller, John M. *The Indian Way*. New York: Macmillan, 1982.

MacIver, Robert M. *The Ramparts We Guard.* New York: Macmillan, 1950.

Mathur, O.P. & Rai, G. "From Existentialism to *Karmayoga*: A Study of Arun Joshi's *The Foreigner*," A.K. Srivastava (ed.), *Alien Voice: Perspectives on Commonwealth Literature.* Lucknow: Print House, 1981.

Mukherjee, Meenakshi. *The Twice Born Fiction: Themes and Techniques of The Indian Novel in English.* New Delhi: Arnold-Heinemann, 1971.

Naik, M.K. *A History of Indian English Literature.* New Delhi: Sahitya Akademi, 1982.

Prasad, Hari Mohan. *Arun Joshi.* New Delhi: Arnold-Heinemann, 1985.

Radhakrishnan, S. (ed. & tr.) *The Bhagavadgita.* New Delhi: Harper Collins Publishers, 1993; rptd. 2000.

Sartre, Jean Paul. *Nausea* (tr.) R. Baldick. Harmondsworth: Penguin, 1965.

Singh, R.S. *Indian Novel in English: A Critical Study.* New Delhi: Arnold Heinemann, 1977.

Verghese, C. Paul. *Problems of Indian Creative Writers in English.* Bombay: Somaiya, 1971.

3

REDEMPTION THROUGH KNOWLEDGE: *THE STRANGE CASE OF BILLY BISWAS*

The second novel of Arun Joshi, *The Strange Case of Billy Biswas* (1971) also revolves round the crisis of self, the resultant agony and Man's quest for affirmation. Though it has some similarities with its predecessor, *The Foreigner*, it is another version of Man's quest for understanding his self by shunning the world (*Maya*) through knowledge (*Jnana*). As *The Foreigner* was inspired by the theory of *Karmayoga*, *The Strange Case* draws its motivation from *Jnanayoga* (The Way of Knowledge). Deeply influenced by the oriental theories, the novel attempts to explore "that mysterious underworld which is the human soul" (Mathai: 8) which has its own angularities and dimensions. The despondency of its protagonist Billy Biswas is the result of his estrangement in modern society and civilization that forces him to take refuge in the world of tribals. That he has the sympathies of his creator also is testified to by the personal touch Joshi gives his novel by dedicating it "To my father/in memory of thirty years of love and friendship." The theme of alienation for finding answers to some perennial questions is dealt with competently by Arun Joshi here. The motif of quest permeates the whole narrative as the novelist himself has admitted in his interview: "My novels are essentially attempts towards a better understanding of the world and of myself" (Bannerjee: 3).

The story is unfolded from the witness-narrator point of view. The narrator Romesh Sahai (Romi) is a friend of the protagonist Billy whom he has met as a student in New York. Romi performs the function of an involved friend and a detached narrator. As the story progresses Romi and Billy get more and more involved and both take the tale to an end. Despite being a concerned friend in Billy's life, Romi finds Billy's character to be an enigma. He disclaims in the beginning of the narrative that he has understood Billy:

> As I grow old, I realize that the most futile cry of man is his impossible wish to be understood. The attempt to understand is probably even more futile. If in spite of this I propose to relate Billy's story, it is not so much because I claim to have understood him as it is on account of a deep and unrelieved sense of wonder that in the middle of the twentieth century, in the heart of Delhi's smart society, there should have lived a man of such extraordinary obsessions (Joshi, 1971: 3).

Romi underlines his modesty still further, "I had neither the imagination nor the obsessive predilection of Billy Biswas" (p. 150). This confession reminds one of Conrad's narrator in *Under Western Eyes* who begins by disclaiming "the possession of those high gifts of imagination and expression which would have enabled my pen to create for the reader the personality of the man who called himself...Razumov" (Conrad: 3). Such statements highlight the dispassionate tone of the novel.

The Strange Case of Billy Biswas starts with depicting Billy as a man of intellect, profound sensibility and unusual obsessions. The son of a judge of Supreme Court of India Billy belongs to a rich and respectable family. His grandfather had been the Prime Minister of a famous princely State in Orissa and his father had practised law at Allahabad and Delhi after completing his law studies. His father had also been an Indian ambassador to a European country. His father sends him to America to take up engineering courses but he starts doing Ph.D. in Anthropology because it is his first love. Billy keeps his father in the dark and specializes as an anthropologist and studies the tribal attitudes and customs. A glance at his library indicates his choicest interests:

> Two of the stacks were devoted exclusively to anthropology. The third presented a melange, that to my mind, made no

> sense at all. It contained every thing from old copies of the *National Geographic Magazine* to the latest pornography that was being pedelled in Times Square: from learned treatise on black magic and witchcraft to a critique of the theory of relativity. What struck me most was a series of nearly forty biographies including several on Van Gogh whose turbulent career, I learnt later, held considerable fascination for Billy at one time. One top of one of the book-cases were piled at least a hundred albums of jazz music. Those were played almost non-stop when he was in the apartment (p. 9).

Romi meets Billy while searching an accommodation in New York. Billy offers to share with Romi his apartment in Harlem, the black colony in America. Though Billy could very well afford to live in some other posh areas like Manhatten; as he comes of an "upper crust of Indian society" (p. 5), he has chosen to live there because, as he tells Romi, he finds it "the most human place" (p. 5). Romi accepts Billy's offer and the sharing of the flat develops into an unusual friendship which lasts till the end.

On the very first day in his room, Billy tells Romi of Avocambo, a play running off Broadway and it gives an insight into the working of his mind:

> It is quite an odd play, really. This chap from New York, quite educated and all that, goes down to the Congo and is so incensed by the heat and the light and the primitive music that he just goes out with his shotgun and starts killing everybody. What is fascinating, of course, are the workings of the deranged mind, what he says between each shot (pp. 6-7).

Billy like the play because "one can quite imagine something like that happening to oneself" (p. 7). It is also significant to note that the anthropologist Van Gogh's turbulent career "held considerable fascination for Billy at one time" (p. 9). Though Billy belongs to the upper crust of Indian society he stays at Harlem because he wants to realize his self to the full. He finds Harlem the only place where he may nurture his sense of belonging by wholly preserving his identity. His constant want to identify himself with his environment is reflected in his aberrant behaviour, his way of living, eating and dressing and even thinking. It is for this that their American host describes Billy as an "anarchist" and "thoroughly crazy even by Indian standards" (p. 5).

The first part of the novel gives us glimpses into Billy's strangeness as a man and also of his liking for the primitive and unsophisticated people. Romi narrates Billy's story in New York and Delhi from his own observations. They are both around twenty two when they meet each other. He is soon impressed by Billy's "almost inhumanly sharp eyes" (p. 39). In America, Billy is drawn towards books on Anthropology and he tells Romi:

> All I want to do in life is to visit the places they describe, meet the people who live there, find out about the aboriginalness of the world (p. 10).

It is around Billy's interest in the primitive life that his entire personality has been structured. Talking to Romi he tells of his "glimpse of the other side:" "Most of us are aware only of the side on which we are born, but there is always the other side, the valley beyond the hills, the hills beyond the valley" (pp. 14-15). This other side concerns the primitive life untouched by sophistication and restraints of the civilized world.

Tuula Lindgren, the Swedish lady of thirty years, who has come to United States for advanced training in psychiatric course and has "extraordinary intuition" (p. 75), understands the dilemma of Billy's life fully. She comes to know what goes in his "dark, unscrutable, unsmiling eyes" (p. 15). She tells Romi that Billy is an extraordinary person and feels inside him a strange force:

> 'A great force, *urkraft*, a...a primitive force. He is afraid of it and tries to suppress it.... 'But it is very strong in him, much stronger than in you or me. It can explode any time' (p. 19).

She finds him "obsessed with a latent quest" (p. 176). Romi on his part notes Billy's urge for the primitive at a music party at

George's apartment. As Billy plays the pair of Bongo drums for nearly quarter of an hour, a hush descends on the atmosphere of the room. Romi and others feel the mesmeric pull of the music which holds everyone by its sheer vitality. The narrator recalls:

> I am certain it was nothing very skilful or sophisticated from the viewpoint of music. What it had, I think, was a mesmeric pull that held us by its sheer vitality. Little packages of sound...falling in one rhythm or another, creating patterns of sound that deep down I knew were not merely that but carried a more fundamental message although what it was I, or Billy for that matter, could not have said. They blazed through our liquor-stimulated sensibilities, like little meteors through the astral night, lighting up landscapes, hills and valleys, gaping charms of the mind that are otherwise forever shrouded in the black mist of the unconscious (p. 17).

It awakens latent primitive urges in the audience and draws towards him a negro girl who sits very close to Billy so that their knees nearly touch. Romi and Tuula are unable to find an explanation for Billy's erratic behaviour. Billy's reply is quite evasive because he says "I must have been disgustingly drunk...what else?" (p. 18) But Romesh's description of Billy's "eating little and talking even less" (p. 20), drinking almost nothing, sitting silently in a corner despite abundance of all that, proves that Billy feels secluded there. He does not drink much to have forgotten himself but makes an effort to attract the attention of the persons at the party. He succeeds in this and soon everybody's eyes are drawn towards him. Even during long walks with Billy, Romi finds his talks "...revealing not only the mind of the speaker but also the dark unknowable layers of the mysterious world that surrounded us" (p. 22). Later he learns from Billy how he often had hallucinations: "It would be like a great blinding flash during which I would be totally unaware of anything else" (p. 179). Tuula with whom Billy discusses his strange dreams, tells him, "in a very mild form such hallucinations occurred in everyone—all art in a way flowed out of them," but she advises him not to "encourage them too much" (p. 179).

The Bhuvaneshwar episode presents Billy's personality to be still more mysterious. He tells Romi how at the age of fourteen, he had experienced the urge to live like a primitive man in the primitive world. He had received the intimations of his primitive self from the moment he emerged from the railway station. He remembers : "It was as though a slumbering part of me had suddenly come awake" (p. 120). It had seemed to him that the sculptures at Konark can give him a solution to his questions about the problem of his anguish and identity: "Who was I? Where had I come from? Where I was going?" (p. 20). If anyone had a clue to it, it was only the *adivasis* who carried about their knowledge in silence, locked behind their dark inscrutable faces (p. 122). One night, he happens to go to the tribal people with his uncle's chauffeur and with deep interest he watches the tribals dancing, drinking, singing and being extremely sensitive, Billy feels a strange sensation:

> First a great shock of erotic energy passed through me, although, mind you, there was nothing particularly erotic about the whole business except once when a boy and a girl, their arm around each other, loitered past me giggling and tumbled into the bush beyond. The shock of erotic energy was followed by the same feeling of unreality or, as I said, a reality sharper than any I had ever known. It was a bit like having taken a dose of hallucinatory drug, something I realized many years later when I was in Mexico... I remember saying: Something has gone wrong with my life. This is where I belong. That is what I have always dreamt of (Emphases added) (p. 123).

While Romi is in America trying to understand Billy's psyche, he receives an urgent message of his father's death. Romi returns to India and after putting in great efforts here he enters the Indian Administrative Service. Billy on the other hand, finds himself itching to be back to India after the completion of his doctoral degree in Anthropology. Even on his return to India, he does not feel homely and temperamentally satisfied at home. A sense of nothingness pervades him. He suffers from a sense of loss of socio-cultural ethos, finds himself in a vacuum which his psyche is unable to comprehend. All this draws upon him when he is standing in a temple at the time of *aarti* (evening prayer):

> I stood before the idols, my hands folded, my head bowed, incense of dhoop tickling my nostrils. I stood there while the pious voices of men, women, and children, rose and fell about me like little waves of a benevolent sea. What I had hoped to achieve by my visit I do not know.... As I stood there, my eyeballs restive behind the quivering lids, it suddenly dawned upon me that it as a all a great waste, that the god who awaited me now was one to which no temples could be built. What awaited me now, I realized was Fate (Emphases added) (pp. 93-94).

It is such moments of awareness that prompt a man take certain decisions to fill the void of his life. Billy's visit to the temple proves that he is trying to adjust himself socially but finds that he is just wasting his time by living in a civilization where people are simply busy making and spending money. This search for viable alternatives lands him as a faculty into Delhi University where he starts undertaking numerous expeditions for coming closer to primitive communities in hills and forests. Billy's antipathy to the city folk and their quality of life is reflected in the following extracts from his letters written to Tuula at different points of time:

> I see a roomful of finely dressed men and women seated on downy sofas and while I am looking at them...they turn into a kennel of dogs yawning yawning (their large teeth showing) or snuggling against each other or holding whisky glasses in their furred paws (p. 92).

> ...the so called thinkers and philosophers and men like that...are hired to find solution, throw light...on complications caused by this making and spending of money (pp. 92-93).

> ...we are swiftly losing what is known as one's grip of life. Why else this constant blurring of reality? Who am I? Who

> are my parents? My wife? My child?...what accident of creation has brought us together (p. 93).

These observations show his concern for civilization, society and individuals including his own self.

In order to overcome his aberrations, Billy decides to get married. He thinks for one moment that marriage would give him a new anchor to cling to and would lead him to an affirmation in life. His marriage to one Meena Biswas, a pretty young daughter of a retired Civil Servant is solemnised. Romi gets another opportunity to mark Billy's bizarre approach when he finds the latter defending before his father the conduct of a clerk who has sacrificed someone else's child to appease the goddess for the recovery of his ailing son:

> Similar cases have been reported from Africa, Indonesia, Japan from even a country like Sweden. As far as India is concerned, there are enough such cases to fill a thousand page volume. Look up the court records of any of the tribal agencies, and you will know what I mean. (p. 50)

He even asserts "there are worlds at the periphery of this one, above it and below it, and around it, of which we know nothing until we are in them" (pp. 50-51). Billy's marriage with Meena turns into a miserable failure. Meena is a product of this 'materialistic' civilization and disappoints Billy who is already disinclined to it. In fact, their marriage is an impulsive action resorted to under the impression that the bond with Meena will be strong enough to bind his split personality. However, it turns out to be otherwise. A product of the money machine culture Meena is worldly wise. She wants nothing but money and glamour which Billy hates. She does not even bother to understand Billy's situation and establish a rapport with him. The marriage of "uneven minds" results in utter failure. Meena's discord with her husband is noticed by Situ, Romi's wife in their very first meeting. The arrogant traits of Meena's character become evident when Situ tells her husband: "Did you see how she looked me up and down?...As if she herself was no less than Miss India or something. Did you notice her hair?" (p. 67). Billy's outburst is very poignant: "the more I tried to tell her what was corroding me, bringing me to the edge of despair so to speak, the more resentful she became" (p. 183).

This domestic strife accentuates Billy's ingrained alienation and he loses temper even at minor issues, quarrelling "all the time," "snapping at everybody" remaining in a "dark mood," not touching his wife for six months, always making fun of Meena, not keeping his promises to his wife and several other things. Meena complains to Romi that "Things are falling apart" (p. 70) and "Billy is getting stranger and stranger with every passing day" (p. 71). Meena hardly initiates moves to improve the situation. She tells Romi: "You see, I just can't handle the situation anymore.... It is all probably my fault. Perhaps I just don't understand him as a wife should" (p. 72). She spies on Billy in an effort to blame his personality: "Tell me Romi, do you think he is having an...an affair" (p. 74). She suggests many solutions to Billy to get rid of her: "Go to your cannibals, if you find me so intolerable" (p. 76) and "I wish I were dead" (p. 76) and further "I will go away if that is what you want" (p. 77). All these murmurs agonise Billy but he replies in a composed mood, "That is not what I want, Meena. You know that" (p. 77) and while saying this Billy finds himself very depressed. In this way Billy's attempt to find a refuge and anchor goes waste. When nearly three years later Romi meets Billy, he finds Billy finished "snuffed out like a candle left in the rain" (p. 66). He says, "Gone was the staggering intelligence, the spectroscopic interests, the sense of humour" (p. 66). It seems to him that the society of Delhi has begun to get on his nerves. Billy tells Romi later:

> What got me was the superficiality, the sense of values. I don't think all city societies are as shallow as ours. I am, of course, talking mainly of the so-called upper classes. I didn't really get to know the others. I don't think I have ever met a more pompous, a more mixed-up lot of people. Artistically, they were dry as dust. Intellectually, they could no better than mechanically mouthed ideas that the West abandoned a generation ago.... Nobody remembered the old songs, or the meaning of the festivals. All the sensuality was gone. So was the poetry. All that was left was

> load-mouthed women and men in three-piece suits dreaming their little adulteries (pp. 176-177).

Utterly disgusted by the external scenario, Billy is gripped by strange hallucinations as he recounts to Tuula, "A strange woman keeps crossing my dreams. I have seen her on the streets of Delhi, nursing a child in the shade of a tree or hauling stone for a rich man's house" (p. 93). Such behaviour leads Romi to infer that Billy's mental condition is "closer to madness, the terrible madness of a man who after great sin and much suffering finally finds himself in the presence of his God" (p. 140). Traces of such abnormality were also noticeable in his American sojourn. At the age of twenty, he had visions "of being in a place other than where I was, in a place very, very old, at times a wilderness, at other times, full of strange primitive people" (p. 123). Such hallucinations continue to haunt him when he teaches at Delhi University. Whenever Billy takes his students for expedition to Central India, he hears an irresistible call from the hills he traverses on. He gives vent to his feelings in one of his letters to Tuula:

> When I return from an expedition, it is days before I can shake off the sounds and smells of the forest. The curious feeling trails me everywhere that I am a visitor from the wilderness to the marts of the Big City and not the other way round (p. 92).

All these happenings affect him greatly. On his last expedition he goes to a tribal village to fetch ropes from the house of the headman of the village, Dhunia, who had become his *Maha prasad* (an intimate friend). Billy had saved the life of his niece by giving her antibiotics on his earlier visit. He meets his niece Bilasia who had now grown into an untamed village beauty. When he leaves for his camp, Dhunia invites him to come next day to watch their dance. When he sleeps in the night he sees a vision and he says it "a dream so erotic, the like of which I did not know could still be conjured up by my unconsciousness" (p. 118). He feels that the whole hilly tract calls him to its primitive fold.

It must be remembered at this point that Billy is not only

sensitive in the literal sense of the term but also conscious of his being. He therefore feels concerned with eternal question of his identity which has been upsetting him since the age of fourteen when he could realize that "something has gone wrong with my life" (p. 123). Given his unhappy experiences, however, he comes to realize that he has been running only after shadowy and illusory appearances. Unable to resist the call of his inner self, he goes to the forest the next night. The call pricks him incessantly:

> Come, come, come, come. Why do you want to go back? Why do you want to go back?... You thought New York was real. You thought New Delhi was your destination. How mistaken you have been: Mistaken and Misled. Come now, come. Take us. Take us until you have had your fill. It is we who are the inheritors of the cosmic night (p. 119).

Billy watches the dance of the tribals and participates in it as well. He drinks the wine and watches all that till it turns into a sort of "orgy" with the feverish beats of drums. He finally decides to abjure the civilized world to join the tribals for ever to find out not only his roots but his identity also. He tells Dhunia the tribal chief, "I am fed up of those slimy bastards who are camped across that river, and I am fed up of the millions who surround me in the wretched city where I come from" (p. 144). Lured by the exciting dance he suddenly finds himself before Bilasia who looks up into his eyes with a smile on her lips: "Her enormous eyes, only a little foggier with drink, poured out a sexuality that was nearly as primeval as the forest that surrounded them" (p. 139). The satisfaction that he gets from Bilasia after mating with her was never given to him before in his life:

> It was that passing moment that rarely comes in a man's life, when he feels that he has suddenly discovered that bit of himself that he has searched for all his life and without which his life is nothing more than the poor reflection of a million others. Bilasia at that moment, was the essence of that primitive force that had called me night after night, year after year (p. 140).

Billy thus leaves the civilized world because he feels suffocated in the phoney atmosphere of the modern society. He rejects the artificiality and hollowness of the sophisticated people totally. Billy appreciates Tuula's treatment of money as 'a whole lot of paper'. In a place like Delhi he feels as if he is "pinned down...like a dead butterfly" (p. 47). He leaves the smart society because he finds his affirmation of the essence of human existence in the primitive life and makes a concerted effort to join an other world away from this civilization. This is not an impulsive action but a well thought out plan. Billy has thought over this question the whole night on that rock beside his tent. His rebellion and abandoning of the city life cannot be termed as a simple case of misunderstanding in his mind. Earlier Billy had indulged himself in finding out his roots and identifying himself with individuals, society, civilization before doing anything like this, but all of them have frustrated his quest. Billy moves out of civilization so mysteriously that he leaves no traces behind. People come to believe that he has been eaten away by a man-eater. Symbolically, it represents the breaking of bonds between the civilized world and Billy. He prefers living with Dhunia, Bilasia and others because he finds here an altogether different atmosphere, "Nobody here is interested in the prices of foodgrains or new seeds or roads or elections and stuff like that" (p. 111). Billy's abandonment of the civilized world is an effort to free himself from external distractions which debar man from attaining detachment from the fruit of action. While stressing on such liberation (inner and outer) Joshi says, "...inner-liberation without detachment is not possible and selfishness is always stopping you from getting liberated. Loneliness is the state where you become aware that you are not liberated and you also do not know how to get liberated" (Piciucco: 91). In a mood of celebration, Billy ponders over reaching the place to which he belonged:

> Had he not known that every four weeks there was a moon like this, that there were hills as blue as these, and people in the hills that were all that he had ever wanted to be. Why did it take him thirty years to discover this. For all his so-called courage, he thought, he, even he, had been afraid,

> afraid and foolish squandering the priceless treasure of his life on that heap of tinsel that passed for civilization (p. 139).

He loves the unrestrained life of the primitive people who go in for drinking and dancing and open orgiastic love making. Contrary to all this are the ways of the upper class sophisticated society which seems to Billy in no way different from those of a kennelful of dogs "yawning or struggling against each other" (p. 92).

The ambition and superficiality of the upper society are represented by Meena, Billy's father, Meena's father and Rima Kaul. Though Billy marries Meena Chatterjee to derive some satisfaction out of his life, he feels a corrupting force working upon him. Meena fails to understand him and they quarrel intermittently. Meena becomes the mother of Billy's child but the emotional gap and lack of understanding prevails. Meena and Billy are not made for each other. According to Romi, Billy's departure might have been avoided if only she had possessed "a rare degree of empathy or even a sufficient idea of human suffering" (p. 183). It is Meena's lack of understanding that out of despair and agony, Billy seduces Rima Kaul, a girl related to Meena. His passions lead him astray and his romance with Rima Kaul is degraded into seduction. One afternoon he takes her to Juhu, hires a room in a third-rate room and seduces her. He remarks: "After it was over I looked into her clear trusting eyes, and I had a first glimpse of my degradation" (p. 186). He behaves in a hypocritical manner even after all this and points out:

> The worst of it was that in spite of this knowledge of my degradation, I continued to behave as before, I continued to whine and lie and sham. I found that I could not stop. I met her three or four times after that. Each time I would determine to be honest—with her, with myself—and each time I would start to play the part as soon as I got the chance... I offered to divorce Meena and marry her even though Rima herself never even hoisted at such a thing. I agreed to start living with her as soon as possible. And all the time I know that I intended no such thing (p. 186).

This experience fills Billy with remorse and he blames the civilized world for this: "It gradually dawned on me that a tremendous corrupting force was working on me. It was as though my soul was taking revenge on me for having denied it for so long that Other Thing that it had been clamouring for" (p. 187). The terrible shock he receives at his degradation instigates his flight from the civilized world. At this point Billy is left in a dilemma what to do. He explains his mysterious disappearance to Romi: "I had two clear choices: I could either follow this call, this vision, whatever the cost, or he condemned to total decay" (p. 188).

Billy decides to go in for the first option viz., following the call of his vision. The tribal girl Bilasia seems to be calling him from the primitive world and Billy falls madly in her love treating her as "the essence of that primitive force that had called me night after night, year after year" (p. 140). Her voluptuousness attracts Billy and the sexual union with Bilasia gives him much satisfaction:

> Her hair was loose. Just behind her left ear there was a red flower. The necklace of beads glowed a little in the darkness.... Come, come, come, she said and Billy Biswas, son of a Supreme Court Justice, went.... It was closer to madness, the terrible madness of a man who after great pain and much suffering finally finds himself in the presence of his god (p. 140).

Billy feels himself at ease in a world devoid of rat race and its resultant miseries. Living among simple people you can "look through their hearts." Even Romi wonders at the relationship of love between the *adivasis* and says: "...I marvelled at the intense beauty of this human relationship that was born out of so much love...." (p. 141). Billy tells Romi the cause of his happiness later: "the earth, the forest, the rainbows, the liquor from the *mahua*, an occasional feast, a lot of dancing and love making, and, more than anything else, no ambition, none at all" (p. 146).

He is very right at this place because it is "ambition" which causes anxiety and rivalry and makes people snobbish.

All types of self-possession come due to ambition which destroys man's values and drives a person to alienation. In the primitive world no "ambition" is to be found. It is this friendly, simple and pure atmosphere that new vistas of knowledge are opened before Billy. The mysterious glow of Chandtola revives to its original after the union of Billy and Bilasia. It seems to us that the whole tribal world is itself waiting for Billy to come and join them. The flame of Chandtola (a peak) had glowed during moonlit nights when the tribal King and the Queen happily lived. It was extinguished when the old King while trying to make the idol of God was poisoned by his relatives. The revival of Chandtola leads to the primitive people that Billy is the reincarnation of their King who was poisoned thousand years ago.

Billy is recognized not only as their King, but is treated as endowed with magical and supernatural powers also. Dhunia (Billy's *Maha prasad*) claims that he has seen Billy send away a tiger who had been roaming in the jungle for a week killing their cattle. He also had brought back Dhunia's grandson to life who had been dead for two hours. All these things remain only sensational ideas for Romi as he never gets a proof for substantiating the veracity of these impressions. But Romi realizes Billy's power of profound faith and unfathomed knowledge when Billy does some improbable things. He predicts rains when there is no sign of relief from the scorching sun. Dhunia aptly informs Romi that Billy "is like rain on parched lands, like balm on a wound. These hills have not seen the like of him since the last of our Kings passed away" (pp. 157-158).

Ten years after his disappearance Billy meets Romi in the jungle. Romi, the district collector of that stretch, is on a tour to the Maikala Range and is startled at Billy's figure when he spots him. Billy is wearing a loin-cloth and is completely tribalized. He attributes his mysterious disappearance to an irresistible urge towards the primitive people and one comes to know about him more clearly.

After this chance meeting Billy keeps on visiting Romi again and again and in the meantime cures Romi's wife Situ's migraine with some herb. Billy takes the promise on the part of Romi that he will not disclose his whereabouts to anybody but Romi's wife Situ forces him to tell her about Billy. Romi fearfully tells Situ and Situ gives out the secret. The tragedy takes place when the so called civilized world impinges upon the world of tribals which provides Billy unusual peace and serenity. In other words, the tragedy takes place when an established man is forced to uproot himself by people whom he hates. It may be noted here that Billy finds himself emotionally attached to Rima so much so that he starts crying when Romi tells him about Rima's death in an accident. Billy is attached to none of his family members, wife, son, and father so Rima's statement that Billy "had nothing to come back to" (p. 87) becomes very significant. When Meena and Billy's father hear about his reappearance, they rush to seek him again. Romesh tries his best to calm down Mr. Biswas and Meena. They do not realize Billy's case and insist on meeting Billy even without his consent. They do not want to lose any opportunity of finding Billy and after Romi's rejection of their requests, Billy's father reports the whole matter to the Chief Secretary who later on threatens to punish Romesh. The orders for searching Billy are given to Rele, the Superintendent of Police, who is no better than an instrument to quell people who revolt against the civilized society. All these people fail to understand Billy's problem and the operation to find out Billy starts. They go to the village where Billy resides with Bilasia and their two sons. None of the villagers is ready to give any clue of Billy's whereabouts. One other news spreads that Billy has killed a constable. The police carries out the combing and ultimately Billy is killed by a hasty bullet of a constable. Billy dies uttering "You bastards" (p. 231). Here Billy's statement shows his contempt for the values of the "civilized world" which does not hesitate to kill him. The tragedy with Billy is that none tries to understand his problem even after his death. All these people think rationally whereas Billy's problem is emotional and is related to his very entity. Mr. Biswas, Meena, Chief Secretary, Rele along with his men and even Situ, Romi's wife stand as Joshi says "only the reprsentatives of a society which, in its middle mediocrity, bracketed men like Billy with irresponsible fools and common criminals and considered it their duty to prevent them from seeking such meagre fulfilment of their destiny as their tortured lives allowed" (pp. 229-30). The constable becomes fearful because he has shot the son of a Supreme Court Judge and Meena without realising her guilt wants the havaldar to be brought to book. None of them realize that Billy indulged in a "search for truth" (p. 175) which is not to be understood by a materialistic people who have sold their souls to Mammon. Romi comments upon the disposal of Billy's case: "it had been disposed of in the only manner that a humdrum society knows of disposing its rebels, its seers, its true lovers" (p. 238). Romi further suggests the result of those who revolt:

> ...nothing but blind blundering vengeance, howsoever camouflaged awaits all those who dare to step out of its strifling confines. It is a confrontation whose outcome is as certain as the end of solitary boats beating against a maelstorm (p. 238).

In this way *The Strange Case of Billy Biswas* portrays how a man of extraordinary obsessions is destroyed by civilization due to his rebellious nature. This story parallels the story of the King of the primitives who staked his life in the hopeless attempt to make the face of God and got nothing. Like *The Foreigner,* this novel is another variation of the doomed existential quest of man for affirmation in an absurd world since life's meaning lies in the "dark mossy labyrinths of the soul that languish forever, hidden from the dazzling light of the Sun" (p. 4). *The Strange Case* presents forth the attraction for the mysterious forces of the Universe like Bilasia, the tribal girl and Billy's quest for his identity which results in the death of Billy Biswas in the end. He seems to be in a perfect knowledge of his destruction as suggested by Romi but the more important factor is that Billy takes refuge in the tribal civilization as the last resort. He seeks his identity with the civilization, society, individuals and in the process feels like losing his own identity. It is only to find out his roots that he goes to the primitive folds which "guarded him as his own" (p. 239) until his reappearance from "the sanctury of the great god of primitive world" (p. 239).

In this way the outward journey performed by Billy Biswas is symbolic of his relentless quest for a personal salvation. His spiritual concern highlights the meaninglessness of our prosperity and civilized society in the first part of the novel when he finds himself alienated from individuals, society and civilization as such. Though Billy goes on putting in efforts to remain a part and parcel of society by pinning his hopes on individuals (the smallest social unit) he fails in every effort. After seducing Rima Kaul, he realises his own degradation and yearns to transcend his life of degradation into a life of life-sustaining values. The burden of his degradation is so great that instead of breaking himself he prefers to abjure the city life and join the tribals. It is in those folds of Maikala Hills that he relieves himself of his burden and finds his identity. The efforts of Meena and Billy's father to get Billy back can be interpreted in terms of attempts to uproot him again from his locale. At this juncture, Billy prefers dying to succumbing to their wish.

The novel is divided into two parts, the first one consisting of about hundred pages and the second one of another one hundred and fifty pages. Both these parts may be named as 'The Civilized World' and 'The Primitive World' respectively. These two worlds represent two distinct cultures which these geographical locations embody. The novel reveals to us the falsity of the so-called refinement of the Indian upper class society. It is obviously anti-bourgeois in taste and "testifies a loss of confidence in the anglicised Indian tradition of high culture" (Prempati: 175) which is the offshoot of the Western culture.

It is remarkable that the novel opens in New York's Harlem, the black ghetto of America. It is a conscious choice on the part of Billy Biswas to take residence in Harlem which cannot be regarded as a dignified place by the middle class standards. It appears that he takes refuge in Harlem after being totally fed up of the dissipation around. He is a rebel from the very beginning. An individual of such temperament defies all theories of rebellion. He vehemently denounces the moral and spiritual degradation of his own culture from which he has come when he says to Romi: "What got me was the superficiality, the sense of values. I don't think all city societies are shallow as ours. I am, of course, talking mainly of the so-called upper classes" (p. 177). Such view hardly comes from a man of negative attitude. When he seduces Rima Kaul in the midst of his quarrels with Meena, his wife, he thinks he would forever hold himself in contempt and remorse for what he has done to Rima. He concludes that he has started to behave in the same manner as the general people of city would have behaved. What makes his condition all the more worse is that Rima is still fond of him and is emotionally attached to him. He hears the voice of his soul scolding him: "Hear you swine, if you haven't the guts to break away from this filth, well, then, I am going to wallow in it until it makes you sick" (p. 187).

The realisation goads him to search for the other thing which is his search for affirmation both physical as well as spiritual: "That other thing was, and is, after all, what my life is all about" (p. 187). Joshi explains it as a mystical drive in Billy Biswas "very often a mystical drive or an erotic drive or a primitive drive are all common. I would say that he had all these three drives at one stage of his life. Anyway, the mystical one seems to be the most important" (Picuicco: 91). Romi fails to understand these big words and asks Billy whether he means his desire to become a primitive. Billy says:

> I don't want to sound too pompous, old chap. Becoming a primitive was only a first step, a means to an end. Of course, I realized it only after I ran away. I realized then that I was seeking something else. I am still seeking something else (p. 187).

Later when Romi asks what was he seeking? Was it God? He reluctantly replies that it was not God but a thing similar to God. Here it becomes clear that he is searching for salvation and affirmation of his self in life.

The novelist has portrayed the primitive girl Bilasia as a foil to the sophisticated Meena Biswas. This contrast colours the central vision of the novel. When Billy sees Bilasia for the first time, she appears to him the essence of that '*urkraft*' that had called Billy night after night. It was to this call he responded in his childhood at Bhuvaneshwar. It was the same force which made Billy so frenzied when the negro girl moved—sexually to him when he played a pair of Bongo drums. Further he blames the same force enacting its revenge on him when he seduced Rima Kaul:

> It was as though a master mind had arranged the whole thing to give me a preview of what awaited me if I continued to defy its call. Poor Rima had crystallized for me the alternatives, although I did not realise this until I sat outside my tent that fateful night (pp. 187-188).

Billy, though born and brought up in the same culture builds his own glass castle because his soul is yearning for affirmation and he cannot compromise with forces opposed to it.

Right from the very beginning, Billy's life is dominated by his visions and hallucinations. He ponders at length on the typically human handicap:

> Sometimes I think the human mind is equipped with a built in apparatus for compromise. As soon as you are faced with a difficult choice this apparatus is switched on. It runs about here and there, brokering between various parts of man, rationalizing this, postponing that, until what is left is the conventional expedients of the age and hardly a choice. Deep down we are afraid that the price of making such choices is terrible, not realizing that the price of not making them is even more terrible (p. 188).

Billy's experience just before his momentous decision to make his final departure into the jungle on the second day of his expedition has apparent mystic undertones. He feels that "the inheritors of the cosmic night" (p. 119) were "waiting and walking and staring" at him and he was the "first man on earth facing the earth's first night" (p. 118). Billy's departure is not an escape from life and its realities but an escape into what he thinks "real life" far from the "madding crowd's ignoble strife." It is there that he experiences the fulfilment of human existence.

Billy presents himself as "a refugee from civilization" (p. 140). The dogged determination which we notice in his search for meaning in an incoherent and chaotic world is a sterling trait of his character. He recapitulates how he could get out of the confusing mess:

> I certainly underwent a deep metamorphosis that was, no doubt, responsible for all that I did subsequently. Layer upon layer was peeled off me until nothing but my primitive self was left trembling.... (p. 119).

Driven by elemental human impulses which are in consonance with his own innate nature Billy's conduct is the manifestation of those organic drives which are at loggerheads with the rational forces: "I had no idea it was going to happen. It was two days—and two nights—before I knew what I had done. By then it was too late" (p. 109).

His rejection of all familial ties tantamounts to renunciation which "has always been an Indian ideal of life" (Mukherjee: 97). The inevitability of events which happen in Billy's life support the metaphysical touch of his quest. His withdrawal from the world is in the nature of a reflex action, he withdraws in order to preserve himself from "those rapacious representatives of civilization." Jasbir Jain rightly comments, "Long before his physical disappearance into the saal forests of the Maikala Hills, he had ceased to belong to the world" (Jain: 54). As Sindi in *The Foreigner* gets his revelation sitting on a "weathered stone," Billy gets it when he meets Bilasia. It is a movement which makes him feel that he "has suddenly discovered that bit of himself that he has searched for all his life and without which his life is nothing more than the poor reflection of a million others" (p. 140).

The Foreigner and *The Strange Case* suggest different approaches to solve life's meaninglessness. *The Foreigner* presents detachment as a possible panacea for life's problems. "I don't want to get involved," says he though "everywhere I turned I saw involvement" (Joshi, 1968: 70). The detachment which he cultivates to overcome his painful memories and meaninglessness of life becomes a source of deeper agony to him. The fault with Sindi lies in his mistaking detachment for inaction but later on he finds that "Detachment consisted of right action and not escape from it" (*Ibid*: 193). The lesson which he takes is "detachment lies in actually getting involved" (*Ibid*: 225). Billy, on the other hand, testifies that if one is able to establish a rapport with nature, one can get rid of all agonies of life. Bilasia represents here "the primitive culture, the untapped subterranean resources of psychic energy" (Srinath, 1979: 39). Further we are reminded that Bilasia is "the embodiment of that primal and invulnerable force, that has ruled these hills (Maikala) perhaps this earth, since time began" (p. 224). Joshi depicts the beauty of Bilasia with an unforgettable mixture of myth and nature:

> ...She had that untamed beauty that comes to flower only in primitive people. It was as though nature were cocking a snook at Meena Biswases of the world, informing them once again how little it cared for their self-proclaimed superiority. Looking at Bilasia one could well believe that these were the children of Kings condemned to exile by those rapacious representatives of civilization who had ruled the thrones of Delhi and still continued to do so. Where else could be found that proud carriage, a figure so graceful, eyes where brightness made your pulse quicken. Where else had I ever seen a grief so tragic that might well have brought tears to the eyes of a stone god (p. 141).

No wonder, time and again Billy recalls the momentous experience: "I arrived at the fork in my life that, without being conscious of it, I had waited for all my life. I took the turning that was as irrevocable as it was awesome. Why all this happened to me I do not know and even if I knew I could not put it into words" (p. 142).

Commenting on the nature of quest-motif, Meenakshi Mukherjee seems to be closer to the heart of the narrative: "It is a compelling novel about a strange quest drawing upon myth and folk-lore to reiterate its elemental concerns" (Mukherjee: 203). Billy possesses an extraordinary vision of a simpler and purer life-style, he complains to Tuula of a "constant blurring of reality" (p. 93). Tuula detects the expression of a primitive force due to which Billy becomes enchanted with the music and dance of the Bhils and with the supernatural charms of the Chandtola peak. The patience of the Bhils is sharply contrasted against the barren pleasures of Delhi "smart set." Billy seeks to identify himself with them by discarding away his western clothes and starts wearing only a loin cloth. Romi notices the transformation of his friend and says: "For all his so called courage, he thought, he...had been afraid, afraid and foolish, squandering the priceless treasure of his life on the heap of tinsel that passed for civilization" (p. 139). As compared to the "heap of tinsel," the value of the vision is superior as Billy himself voices to the narrator: "The essence of life, it seems to me, can be communicated only in the language of visions and what vision has lasted a period even as short as a man's life" (p. 140). Billy unconsciously dwells on the perennial human situation which defies artificial barriers:

> What kept us happy, I suppose, were the same things that kept all primitives happy through the ages: the earth, the forest, the rainbows...an occasional feast, a lot of dancing and love making, and more than anything else, no ambition, none at all (p. 146).

Arun Joshi has very remarkably maintained the contrast between the impulsive behaviour of Billy and the cool account of Romi, the collector friend of Billy. The novel begins with a very humane relationship between these two Indian students in America, Bimal Biswas and Romesh Sahai. The novelist has placed them in an American setting to convince the readers that a great force, "*urkraft*" as Tuula puts it, is very strong in him and even an expensive schooling and his exposure to a highly civilized and modern western society cannot destroy or overcome that force that possesses him completely. His following observation communicated in one of his letters to Tuula is very revealing:

> I sometimes wonder whether civilisation is anything more than making and spending of money. What else does the civilised man do? And if there are those who are not busy earning and spending—the so-called thinkers and philosophers and men like that—they are merely hired to find solution, throw light, as they say, on complications caused by this making and spending of money (pp. 92-93).

As a part of technique, Billy's letters betray the inner mossy labyrinths of his personality. It is these private thoughts that show the working of his mind which is obsessed with ethered concerns. The path chosen by Billy Biswas is obviously the way of *Jnanayoga* (the way of knowledge). His renunciation is an effort to free himself from all desires, longings and egotism which is a pre-requisite for man to attain peace in the way of knowledge. His "becoming a primitive was only a first step, a means to an end" (p. 187) that takes him to liberation at the end. The way of *Jnana* is different from the way of *Karma* (action). It requires us to renounce action and achieve wisdom through meditation, intuition and righteous living. It propounds that man is bound by *karma* and is saved by knowledge. It, therefore, advocates *sanyasa* in which the seeker is directed to eliminate his ego, attenuate his desires and remove his ignorance (*avidya*) which are impediments in his affirmation. As S. Radhakrishnan puts it:

> To get the existential experience of the self, we should get free from the diversity of objects, external and internal, which impedes and prevents the direct or intuitive vision of the essence of the self (Radhakrishnan: 57).

These traits are present in the person of Billy Biswas. His assertion that "I am still seeking something else" like God (p. 187) makes him a true seeker for affirmation through the way of knowledge. His life among tribals is free from desire, anger, ambition, ego and deception that grip the city folk. It has purity and peace that seldom comes in the way of the civilized world.

In fact, the entire novel is an attempt to discuss Billy's instinctive yearning for affirmation. It is not merely the events of his life that the narrator recounts but he also tries to find the truth hidden behind them. So, instead of a straightforward narration of events in their chronological order, the narrator deals with introspective memories, in most thoughts and feelings, intimate human relations, personal letters and discussions. The discussions with Rima Kaul who is head over heels in love with Billy, with Bilasia, with the nosy little fellow from Patna, all serve this purpose. The discussions with Dhunia, the tribal headman explains the psychological impact made by Kala Pahar on Billy which forms the foundation of the novel: "You see what you can when you are awake, and what you cannot see when you are awake comes to you in dreams. It is all the same" (p. 150). The words "strange" and "case" in the title have serious implications. Billy's case is strange because in a world where everyone is running after money and its comforts, Billy though belonging to the upper strata of the Delhi society, opts out of it to achieve affirmation and meaning in his life. He is very much similar to the sages and "*rishis*" in the past who had renounced civilization for the primitive life as a means of realising the truth and God. For psychoanalysts and psychiatrists, he may be a case for study and analysis. His predicament is peculiar and his search is a search for the hidden meaning behind his existence. The title also suggests the civilized world's comment on Billy's behaviour which to the conformists might look as "strange."

The action of the novel has a definite movement. The narrator looks back at his life and events in America and India to juxtapose the natue of experiences. Billy's death at the hands of the humdrum world provides pathos to the story. Though he is regarded as a mythical King by the tribals, his death is a loss only to his immediate relatives and Romi who tries to understand him. The second phase of the novel begins with Billy's appearance in front of Romi and hence forward, the novel moves steadily to a purposeful end. The theme of the novel is embodied in the couplet cited on the opening page—

> I came a thousand miles to see your face, O mountain,
> A thousand miles did I come to see your face.

Though the novel runs along existential lines, it strives to assert much needed values. In a way the novel speaks for spiritual realisation in contrast to mundane entanglements. One observes this when the novel opens in New York's Harlem against some posh American localities and ends in Satpura Hills which stands as a contrast to New Delhi's smart set. These two geographic locations tellingly suggest the quality of life which they represent along with their hazards or otherwise. The complexity of the novel is substantially based on parallelism and contrast. Though Arun Joshi does not use symbols in any significant way here, we can find few events and happenings which seem to be symbolic. Romi, Billy and his uncle stand watching the kites and one of them is cut off from its root and falls somewhere in the big city. This might be taken to symbolise Billy's disappearance from the civilized world. "Bongo drums" and "ghungroos" stand for the inner instincts in Billy.

The novel deviates slightly from *The Foreigner* in the end as Sindi Oberoi finds his meaning in the civilized world itself and learns to live like a *Karmayogi* whereas Billy derives his meaning only after renouncing his city life and joining the primitive world for pure and righteous living. The modern civilization is presented as a great usurper of souls and Billy strives to find out viable alternatives for "the most futile cry of man,...in...smart society" (p. 3). Arun Joshi's third novel *The Apprentice* centres around yet another approach to life viz. devotion (*Bhakti)* to be examined in the next chapter.

WORKS CITED

Bannerjee, Purabi. "A Winner's Secrets," *The Sunday Statesman* (Calcutta), 27 Feb. 1983, 4.

Conrad, Joseph. *Under Western Eyes*. New York: Doubleday and Co., 1925.

Jain, Jasbir. "Foreigners and Strangers: Arun Joshi's Heroes," *Journal of Indian Writing in English*. 5, 1(1977), 52-57.

Joshi, Arun. *The Foreigner*. New Delhi: Hind Pocket Books, 1968; rptd. Orient Paperbacks, 1993.

——. *The Strange Case of Billy Biswas*. New Delhi: Asia Publishing House, 1971. All citations refer to this edition followed by paginations.

Mathai, Sujata. "I am a Stranger to My Books," *The Times of India* (Bombay), 10 July 1983, 8.

Mukherjee, Meenakshi. *The Twice Born Fiction*. New Delhi: Arnold-Heinemann, 1971.

Piciucco, Pier Paolo. "An Interview with Arun Joshi," *Journal of Indian Writing In English*. 25, 1-2 (1997), 87-95.

Prempati, D. "*The Strange Case of Billy Biswas:* A Serious Response to a Big Challenge," R.K. Dhawan (ed.), *The Fictional World of Arun Joshi*. New Delhi: Classical Publishing Co., 1986.

Radhakrishnan, S. (ed. & tr.). *The Bhagavadgita*. New Delhi: Harper Collins Publishers, 1993; rptd., 2000.

Srinath, C.N. "Crisis of Identity: Assertion and Withdrawal in Naipaul & Arun Joshi" his (ed.). *The Literary Landscape*. Delhi: Mittal Publications, 1986.

4

Redemption Through Devotion: *The Apprentice*

Arun Joshi's next novel *The Apprentice* (1974) is cast in the form of a dramatic monologue similar to that of Camus's *The Fall*. Like Sindi in *The Foreigner* and Billy in *The Strange Case*, Ratan Rathor the protagonist is yet another reflective introvert. His problem is to educate himself so that he may unravel the labyrinths of life. *The Apprentice* also probes deeper into the inner consciousness of the individual with a view to explore what Arun Joshi calls "that mysterious underworld which is the human soul" (Mathai: 8). Ratan seems to be a victim of the "petrified and frozen" society of the modern world throughout the novel and the plot is woven round his memories of events that take him out of a village and enable him secure a foothold in the metropolis of Delhi.

The protagonist Ratan like Jean-Baptiste-Clamence, the narrator of *The Fall*, discloses the secret of his existence because his conscience exhorts him to expiate his sins of cowardice and dishonesty by exposing his own character in a mocking manner. He is a thoroughly existentialist character who exemplifies the doctrine that man's salvation depends upon the course of life he chooses to lead. He is neither a rebel like Billy Biswas nor a rootless foreigner like Sindi. He is a practical man whose idealism is shattered by the corruption in society. The social scenario of the post-independence period becomes the background of the novel and Ratan is torn between conflicting ideologies like idealism and corruption and consequently after much suffering reaches a sort of salvation at the end when he decides to clean up the shoes of visitors at a temple gate. In fact,

"The novel enacts three stages in the human divine comedy of Ratan. The pre-Independence period is the dawn, the period of idealism, the phase of innocence, the post-Independence India is the broad daylight of experience, the inferno of corruption, the last part the area of expiation, is the door to the purgatory" (Prasad: 60). After reaching this last stage, Ratan confesses to a silent listener—a student who has come from Punjab to Delhi to rehearse for the N.C.C. Parade on Republic Day. At the time of confession Ratan is a senior official in the Ministry of Defence and tells the listener about his father's death under the British regime, his hunt for a job, his marriage with his boss's niece, his industrious life and lastly the deed of accepting a bribe for clearing the defective war material during China invasion. Ratan further tells him the miserable plight of his only friend, a Brigadier in the Army which compels him to examine the entire stance of his life.

If its predecessor is dedicated 'To my father,' *The Apprentice* is "To/My Mother" and this fact lends a personal ambience to the plot of the novel. Ratan is a child of double inheritance—the patriotic and ideal world of his father and the worldly selfish and sagacious universe of his mother. His father though an advocate, who gave up his legal profession, was suffused with patriotic zeal and to eventually sacrifice his life as a believer in the Gandhian creed of non-violence. He was shot dead by a British Sergeant while leading a procession of freedom fighters. Ratan has tenaciously nursed his father's ideals but his sudden death creates a problem of alarming proportions for him. His mother brings him face to face with the horrible reality of materialistic society:

> "Don't fool yourself son, she said. Man without money was a man without worth. Many things were great in life, but the greatest of them all was money" (Joshi, 1974: 19).

His mother believes that Ratan's inclination to follow his father's ideals was nothing but madness:

> It was not patriotism but money that brought respect and bought security. Money made friends. Money succeeded where all else failed. There were many laws, but money was law unto itself (p. 19).

Maturing as he has been emulating his father's lofty ideals, Ratan gets stunned into silence at his mother's advice. The sudden awareness that money is the most important determinant of human situation—"law unto itself"—is treated by Ratan as a vision, the guiding principle of life. He regards it as if it were the ultimate truth uttered by some divine power in the form of his mother:

> It was as though an oracle had spoken and revealed to me the mystery of the Universe. I felt very sad and helpless. I felt as though I had lost all control over my destiny which from then on would be governed not by what I worked for or how good I was put by some intricate laws of money of which I had no knowledge (p. 19).

When Ratan comes out of the college after passing his exams and struggles for a job, he soon discovers that the honour of being the son of a freedom fighter is of no practical value. His father's sacrifice for the cause of national freedom has left behind only suffering for his survivors. His mother has been suffering from tuberculosis and can not be properly treated for want of money. He undergoes several humiliating experiences while looking for a job. His intelligence and education do not come to his rescue. At this point Ratan finds himself in a shocked position:

> ...What is more shattering than the breakdown of a faith?.... What hurts is the collapse of the faith that they destroy. You believe there is justice in the world. You go about the world for fifty years, this belief sitting in your heart. Then something happens and you go seeking justice. And justice is not there. Or, you assume your wife is faithful, your children love you, your boss fair, or that God exists. And then some day proof comes along that nothing is so. This is what hurts (p. 23).

Ratan tries hard to get a job in Delhi while staying at a *Sarai* but all his resources fail and are of no avail. The depressing experiences of job-hunting, of being "examined, interviewed, interrogated, and rejected" (p. 29) have a crushing effect on him. Having only a little money at his disposal, he stays in a room with five other workers. He remains always apprehensive of his failure: “What got me down, wiped the laughter off my face, so to speak, was that they worked, earned, spent and I had no job. I, who was the most educated of them all, would soon be on the streets, a failure, an incompetent, penniless fool” (p. 25). To command respect of his room-mates, he takes recourse to lying and thus adds “a new dimension to my life. I had become, at the age of twenty-one, a hypocrite and a liar; in short, a sham...I had become a master faker. And all this had happened within a period of six weeks” (p. 27). This gives his values the first major blow and all paradigms of noble life start shattering before him. With the passage of time Ratan becomes a past master in keeping up appearances. Even common human decency and courtesy is thrown to the winds. Once he falls ill and is helped by those very room-mates whom he does not like much. He narrowly escapes death after falling a victim of sun-stroke only with the help of the turner and the two Mirjapur brothers. When he recovers, a chance introduction by the stenographer secures him a job of a temporary clerk in the department of war purchases. From that day Ratan never looks back. He even surprises himself by ignoring those who had saved him from death. After a chance remark of his boss about the place where Ratan lives, he abandons his lodgings without even waiting to say good-bye to the turner who was away on the evening shift. In this way a remarkable change in Ratan’s character is perceptible which is hardly in conformity with his upbringing. The early faithfulness has given place to practicality and slowly and gradually he is going to become a part of the ‘bourgeois filth’ (p. 39) which his father used to denigrate. He recapitulates: “I have remembered this. But remembering is not believing my friend or, believing doing. When the moment comes we only remember what best grinds our axe” (p. 32).

Now onwards Ratan’s only aim is to make his career: “educated, intelligent, cultured, and it was my right that I should rise in life, to levels higher than others aspired for” (p. 32). He thinks of his officer, the Superintendent closer to a pontiff or a high priest of an exclusive cult who becomes a key to his career. A peculiar instinct for survival overwhelms him and he works "harder than almost anybody in the department except the Superintendent himself" (p. 35). With the help of his obedience and docility he wins the confidence of the Superintendent who later on confirms his job. His journey as an office clerk begins and further corruption of his soul is only a matter of time. Though at times he contemplates:

> I embarked upon the solemn and relentless pursuit of a career. Bourgeois filth, careers and bourgeois filth... There have been moments in my life when I saw nothing but filth around me. At such times my head would explode with violent, rebellious thoughts. But when I would always calm down, and ask myself: What can be done? Here I am. And here is the filth. What can I do? How can I get away?... One had to live. And, to live, one had to make a living. And, how was living to be made except through careers (p. 39).

Since Ratan has embarked on building a career, he has to agree to marry his boss's niece. He loses his identity and becomes "a thick-skin and a washout" (p. 41). By now he knows that the world runs on the basis of deals and "if men forgot how to make deals the world would come to a stop...it is not the atom or the sun or God or sex that lies at the heart of the universe: it is DEALS" (p. 48). He becomes a modern man in the full sense of the term—cunning, deceptive, selfish and easy-going. He goes to bring his mother to see the girl he has to marry knowing full well that her consent is mere a formality and feels that his marriage has also been degraded into a deal. The night in the train while going to call his mother becomes a painful nightmare for him. He suffers from humiliation and cannot sleep for many nights: "...nights of humiliation, nights when you are ashamed of something, ashamed of yourself, when the darkness is full of insults, pointing fingers and mocking laughter" (p. 47).

While undergoing such a conflicting situation of conflict between the higher ideals of his father and his instinct for survival in the modern world, Ratan exercises his "choice" to pursue his material ends on the Sartrean line of existentialistic ideology. After his marriage, Ratan becomes an officer within a couple of days of India becoming a Republic. Though he rises in life through corrupt practices, he is far from achieving satisfaction. He now owns a car, a flat of his own, a refrigerator and has twenty thousand rupees in the bank. The higher he rises the more unscrupulous, fraudulent and hypocritical he becomes: "The more money I accumulated, the more I was dissatisfied and the more I was determined to 'enjoy' life. And all the time I thought of death" (p. 85).

Quite contrary to such a stand in his life, Ratan feels strongly for his motherland, when the Indo-China War starts. He frequently recollects his father's ideals and calls his behaviour at this moment exemplary. He always talks about the miserable condition of the country. He meditates as to who should be held responsible for the debacle of war: the ill-equipped military or the incompetence of the politicians. After much deliberation Ratan concludes that the root of the downfall was not the military, nor the politicians, nor the weather but the "INDIAN CHARACTER" (p. 55). With a view to bringing about a change in the existing set-up, Ratan writes an essay on the "Crisis of Character" in which he hits at the corruption in society and describes Indian people as "a glorious monument in ruin, a monument of which even the foundations had caught canker" (p. 50). A merry fellow calls him "Mr. Crisis of character" but this does not weaken his enthusiasm. In spite of his promotion and material gains, he does not feel at home in such a corrupt atmosphere though "he has been gradually sinking into the abyss of darkness of corruption, exploitation and bourgeois filth" (Das: 41) and he has satisfaction of swimming and not sinking.

In such an agonised conscience Ratan meets Himmat Singh, the Sheikh who offers him a big bribe and tempts him into a big bargain for the supply of defective war materials to the Army. Ratan stoops low little realising the fact that it is related to the security of his country. He derives courage from his observation that everyone is busy amassing wealth by exploiting the opportunities thrown out by the war. He watches with utter dismay that people have started hoarding commodities such as baby food and antibiotics to sell them on much profit at the time of war. He approves of the defective war material which results in the death of his own friend, the Brigadier. It is only later that he realises his blemish: "What happened to me during that time and this? That is what I ask myself time and again without getting an answer" (p. 59) and "How could men who had burnt away twenty years of their lives for a cause do things that would so surely make a wreck of it? How could they possibly change so suddenly?" (p. 60). He blames the prevailing atmosphere for his degradation. He finds himself trapped in the corrupt system where "men were weighed in Money or Power" (p. 62) limiting his option. His freedom has no meaning and it seems to be nothing but a word, "Freedom. Freedom. What is freedom but a word, my friend? Freedom of men, of nations. No more than a word... We thought we were free. What we had, in fact, was a new slavery with new masters" (pp. 60-61). He wonders how he can be his own master when he has been smothered by a system. He justifies his action vehemently:

> If I had taken a bribe I belonged rather to the rule than the excepton. Peons were frequently taking bribes. So were government officials and traffic policemen and railway conductors. A bribe could get you a bed in a hospital, a place to burn your dead. Doctors had a fee to give false certificates, magistrates for false judgements. For a sum of money politicians changed sides. For a larger sum they declared wars. Bribery was accepted by factory inspectors, bank agents and college professors; by nurses, priests and chartered accountants; by all those who acted in the public interest. Men took bribes to facilitate the seduction of their wives; women for seduction of other women. All this I knew and had known for twenty years (pp. 108-9).

Ratan becomes obsessed with wealth and sacrifices the principles that have guided him during adolescence, a complete diversion from the ideals and morals dear to his mind and heart in youth. He calls himself a nobody without any identity:

> I was a nobody. A NOBODY. Deep down I was convinced that I had lost significance; As an official; as a citizen; as a man. How could then my actions have significance? What significance was there in steering a boat that had no

> destination or watering a tree that would never bear fruit (p. 70).

This realisation is just momentary. When he goes to Bombay to sign the agreement related to defective war materials, another change is seen in his behaviour as he is drawn to wine and women. So far he had lacked courage to give vent to his physical desires but acquisition of wealth has emboldened him: "I felt bold, unfettered. I stared at them, the women. Openly, wilfully. To the point of rudeness. What is interesting is that not only did I stare at them but I felt that I had a right to stare...I felt confident" (p. 74). Ratan visits prostitutes as well and realises later that "I was, in fact, at the peak of dung heap that I had been climbing all my life" (p. 82).

Ratan's visit to Bombay, "a city reclaimed from the Sea for purposes no other than that of commerce" (p. 76) gives him the knowledge that even a Member of Parliament, "a trustee of the Republic" (p. 86) is not worried at all about the fate of war: "Nobody lost a war these days, the M.P. said. There were always compromises. To be candid, he whispered, who cared for the wilderness that we were quarrelling over" (p. 82). Ratan is surprised to know that the Sheikh "conducts his operations for neither money nor power but in order only to destroy" (p. 81), and derives sadistic pleasure in destroying "Everything from top to bottom, fron one end of the continent to the other" (p. 77). Before signing the deal Ratan shows some unwillingness for the fear "that people would come to know", but Sheikh tells him that only fools like him believe there is a law book laid down by God which they must follow: "There was no such book, Rathor—What existed—was not written by God but by a silly society that would do anything for money" (p. 72). He further tells Ratan: "This country had two kinds of people—the rulers and the ruled" (p. 80). The rulers were a fraud phoney people who know only how to make speeches, be cruel and feather their nests, and who made a mess of things without knowing how to clean it up. The ruled were "brainless" (p. 80). All this disturbs Ratan and it leaves him with the old depressing feeling that something had gone wrong with his life. His existence is tormented by the question "Why did I take the bribe?" (p. 61) because he feels that he has accepted the bribe when he really does not need money. His similarity with Camus's Jean-Baptiste-Clamence can be seen when he says: "Yet I was unhappy about this as if I had violated the code of honour" (Camus: 47).

Unfortunately Ratan's experience in Bombay at the party and in the brothel corrupts him so much that he reaches a point of no return. He is in a pitiable plight—"restless, depressed, uncomfortable" (p. 66). He further says: "Many things disturbed me but where I had expected new achievements, new standards, there were no standards. No standards at all" (p. 63). He has violated the path shown by his father by becoming a pawn in the hands of some corrupt people while the latter sacrificed his life for the sake of the country:

> I was no fornificator. I was the son of a revolutionary born to lead revolution. If not lead them, at least to be a part of them. I came from a race of men who had, over thousand years, battled for honour. I was expected to make sacrifices if required, give up my life for a noble cause. In all this I had obviously failed. The failure could perhaps be overlooked. But I was at least required to be good, sensible, uphold decency, preserve a sense of shame. At the least I was expected to think of my wife and my marriageable daughter. In short, I was expected to behave (p. 85).

The agonised state of Ratan's mind results in his physical ailments. He himself observes slouch in his spine, as his body bends to one side. He loses physical briskness and feels used up. He contrasts himself with his father and the Superintendent who had been his inspirations once:

> For some reason this disfigurement of posture disturbed me. The best men in my life—my father, the Superintendent, the Brigadier had possessed a physical briskness that had marked them out from the crowd, a briskness that I had envied and emulated. Not without success. I too, at one time, had been complimented on my demeanour and here I was slouching and yawning every five minutes of a crisp winter morning. It was rarely that I

> had seen those men yawn except when they were ready to go to sleep or something (pp. 63-64).

He feels self-betrayed as well. His moral dilemma reduces him to "the status of those leaves of autumn that are blown here and there, at the mercy of the wind" (p. 69). His frail and fragile existence is shaken by the most tormenting question: "What else can I tell you that would explain my act, why I took the bribe?" (p. 69). His guilty conscience meets the existential heroes of Joseph Conrad, Graham Greene and William Golding "in the sense that the act of treachery inflicts an irreparable injury upon the moral nature of man, and that a guilty Ratan lives inescapably in the presence of his conscience. He too realises, as Razumov does in Conrad's *Under Western Eyes,* that all a man can betray is his conscience" (Das: 43). Ratan becomes a typical modern man and Joshi has made him "at once every man and nobody" (Barret: 5). In utter confusion he feels fed up with the life of hypocrisy, deception and all round corruption and becomes isolated and estranged from society. He says:

> How, all these years, I have been alone, so horribly alone in my anger, in my failures, carrying them in secret, like a thief, close to my heart, until their blazes have turned upon me and turned me to ashes. Believe me, I have seen it happen. I have seen my soul turn to ashes (p. 71).

Joshi's description of Ratan's "soul turn to ashes" is a proof of his moral degradation and isolation. It is due to all this that in spite of all the luxuries, he is not happy in his life. One evening when he sits by the side of his wife inside the temple before the statue of God, he feels unnerved and speaks utterly disturbed:

> That evening, as I sat with my wife at the temple before the great God, the God of courage and renunciation, that evening as I sat vowing and watering at the mouth before this great God I was already beyond his pale (p. 69).

His wife is also unsatisfied in spite of their luxurious life and material prosperity. Ratan comments with a feeling of irreparable loss: "But why blame my wife? It is true her discontent got on my nerves, rather unnerved me. It created for me a perpetual disturbance, the nagging feeling that our lives had been robbed of an essential substance..." (p. 69). Becoming painfully aware of having lost "an essential substance" of life, he like an existential hero cries out in utter despair: "What had I done, what had I done which I should not have done? What was right, what was wrong? What was the measure for doing things or not doing them? What were the dividing lines: between success and failure, loyalty and betrayal, love and hate?" (p. 69).

After the Bombay episode we come to learn of the return of his Brigadier friend from the fighting fronts of Indo-China war. The war is lost and the Brigadier, upon his return from the battlefront is suffering from nervous breakdown. When Ratan goes to visit him, he finds the Brigadier terribly shocked and emaciated: "The man whom I always looked up to and who had been the nicest to me was in panic, sacred out of his wits" (p. 90). The Brigadier is taken to the hospital and admitted in Emergency Ward. It is worth stating that during their childhood days, the Brigadier had saved Ratan's life when he was attacked by a group of hooligans. The Brigadier had leapt across the fallen bicycles to "fight for me, me who no one had ever fought for" (p. 17). It is the irony of Fate that Ratan himself becomes responsible for the Brigadier's retreat from the war front and the consequent nervous breakdown. Ratan is horrified to see his friend in such a condition: "I watched him with a sense of doom. And watching him I remembered the autumn evenings on an athlete field and in the growing dusk the cry of the nightingales.... It was the second time in my life that I had felt the pain of another as my own, the first being the time when my father was shot" (p. 100).

When Ratan is called by the Superintendent of Police for interrogation, he deceives him by saying that he has no knowledge about the clearnance of the defective war materials which has caused the loss of several hundred lives. His reaction is full of surprise and of great indignation. He answers like a confirmed hypocrite and shows great self-righteousness and shock that at the hour of national peril someone should do this. They tell him that they had plenty of evidence that he has cleared those war materials. Ratan is put into the police custody and he is filled with amazement at the sorry state of his affairs:

> I watched his disappearing back in a daze of disbelief. Was it a dream, a nightmare, hallucination caused by some poisonous drug? Or, was I not Ratan Rathor, an official of the Government of India but someone else, someone born of criminal parents dragged out of the slums of the old city? If I was not Ratan Rathor, what was I? Was I a thief? A scoundrel? Was I the murderer, they said I was? (p. 106).

While sitting on a stool in the small room at the police station, Ratan thinks of the after effect when people will come to know about his vile deeds. There is a conflict in his conscience whether he should confess or deny the allegations. He thinks of Honour, *Dharma, Maryada* and their values in life but lastly he makes up his mind not to confess because the authorities have no proof thereof. He goes on keeping a record of several cases of corruption where the guilty have got scot-free: "I thought with satisfaction of a recent fraud executed by the scion of one of the country's secrets for a mistress" (p. 112).

As he is directly responsible for the Brigadier's retreat, his conscience pricks him all the time. He is completely broken at this coincidence that the burden to save the Brigadier should have fallen on him and not on some other man. The S.P. calls him the next day for confession if he so wishes. The following night various thoughts ravage Ratan's mind and he spends sleepless nights thinking about his response to the situation. The result again is the same. He is adamant not to confess though he is aware of his baseness and downfall. He says:

> For twenty years I had lived in this city and for twenty years, it seemed to me, there had been nothing but darkness. And I tried to find home in the darkness. I had stampeded about, lured by carrots regulated by sticks, running here and there without knowing what I sought. Below me, lost in the darkness lay the defeated city. And I thought: The city is defeated, finished. Forget about it. You might have contributed to its downfall. But what had happened has happened. What good is it now to whimper, to confess? (p. 116).

In order to seek peace and moral courage, Ratan visits the temple which is nearby his house. He reaches there at the time of *Aarti* and prays to Lord Krishna to give him strength to confess his crime as diverse thoughts have muddled his head, "I cried. Help me, O God, help me. I am in trouble and I have come to your door. Give me refuge. Give me courage. Just for a day lead me courage. Help me" (p. 118). It can be seen that Ratan is entirely in the grip of duplicity, deception, selfishness and immorality prevailing in the modern society. From the temple he comes to his office and writes his letter of confession. He decides to meet the S.P. in the evening but later on we see that he does not confess at all. In the meanwhile, the Brigadier kills him by shooting in the head and this incident shakes Ratan to his roots:

> Deep down I was convinced that I had lost my significance: As an official: as a citizen: as a man—they wanted this. Did they ever stop to think what I wanted. What right they had to claim my loyalties, take me for granted? What right? Oh, how I have hated THEM at times. And hated myself (pp. 73-74).

Ratan deliberates upon the entire affair afresh and holds Himmat Singh responsible for his one time benefactor and friend's death. He goes to the Sheikh to take revenge upon him and charges the latter for seducing him to this evil. On this the Sheikh retorts: "You are bogus, Ratan Rathor—Bogus. From top to bottom. Your work, your religion, your friendship, your honour, nothing but a pile of dung. Nothing—but poses a bundle of shams" (p. 131). He chides Ratan that one should not blame others for one's own misdeeds and their fallouts. He also explains that Ratan alone has not been responsible for the deal and that there is a big racket involved in the deal, the Secretary and the Minister besides them, and that he has been made a scapegoat only because he is "a spineless flunkey" (p. 136). The Sheikh reveals to him that it is the callous and corrupt society that has made his (the Sheikh's) mother a whore and his sister a vagrant, and that he has been forced to adopt devilish ways by social compulsions. By all these revelations, Ratan understands the absurdity of his existence and reflects on his situation:

"—that I saw more of myself that I had seen before. I did not yet know what had happened to me but one thing was clear: my life had been a great, great waste" (p. 135).

Ratan's visit to the temple to seek peace and solace within and without exposes him to the fact that even religion is not free from corruption. He meets the priest who is ready to grease his (Ratan's) palm to save his son who has used substandard material in the construction of some houses and is now put into prison. In this way Joshi presents India as a nation plunged into corruption. God can be propitiated by gifts in black money to his temples and the priests are themselves corrupt as Ratan sees for himself. As he looks back, he finds, "the grey evening stretched back twenty years until it seemed to me that there had never been sunshine, that for two decades I had lived only in smog: confused, exploited, deceiving, and now deceived. Deceived beyond imagination" (p. 133). Now the difference between a good man and a successful man is clear to him. He comes to know that there is no limit to human depravity. The dead Brigadier's vision pursues him wherever he goes. Ratan is filled with endless remorse and his conscience goes on pricking him every now and then and it alienates Ratan from the degeneratee society as he takes stock of the situation: "Twenty years and nothing gained. An empty life-time. What had I learned? Pushing files? Manoeuvring? At forty five all that I know was to manoeuvre. A trickster, that was what I had let life make of me. Did I know the meaning of honour, friendship? Did I ever know it? Would I ever know it again?" (p. 133). Ratan remembers his ideals and goals when he had come in the metropolis of Delhi twenty years earlier: "Twenty years earlier I had come to this city, just as you have come now; to learn, to work, and in the process to make a mark. I had come full of hope, ambitions, goodwill; and all that was left was a pile of dung" (p. 133).

Although Ratan has sought "solace from the annals of corruption," at every stage he has put up an initial resistance but his efforts have become totally futile. He has always planned to pursue the right path but was invariably distracted into a reprehensible proposition:

> No one seemed to be sure. Whether what was right was practicable. That was where the rub lay. In the practicability of things. That was where I saw the best of them buckle. Because very often the best did not have the daring or the greed of the charlantans. Thus the charlantans won. And when they saw the charlantans winning the best became even less sure of themselves. And at times they turned charlantans (p. 64).

These lines of existentialist wisdom sum up the problem of every individual. "He is caught in the dark labyrinth of life and is unable to follow the light that is within him" (Mathur and Rai: 148). Disillusioned and frustrated as Ratan is, he interprets life in terms of algebra:

> Life more than ever, reminds me of those complex sums in algebra that we do in high school, sums involving twenty equations, all directed at discovering the missing X with which they are in some way related. But they are also related among themselves, acting upon themselves, holding each other up, at times destroying each other and, in the process, the mysterious X. And, at times, they are strongly set up so that the mysterious X is never found, or they are short by one or two and there can be no question of finding X, try as you might (p. 49).

Such a realisation is "the apex of existential wisdom" (Thakur: 162). He holds himself responsible for the betrayal of his spirit and confess to Himmat Singh: "That is a terrible sensation—the realisation that one's life has been a total waste, a great mistake; without purpose, without results. There are many sorrows in the world, but there is nothing in the three worlds to match the sorrow of a wasted life. All else, thoughts of revenge, of pleasure, of pain, pale before it, are made pointless" (p. 135).

Ratan is not sure as to how all this has happened. How the entire atmosphere of society has gone corrupt. He feels like doing something to change the prevailing situation though feels diffident to rid the society of this pestilence. He learns that one cannot live for oneself because no human act is performed in isolation and therefore each act should be done with a sense of responsibility. With a deep urge to undergo penance and affirm his life, Ratan undergoes the sternest apprenticeship of its own quality in the world. He starts from the very lowest by dusting the shoes of the congregation outside the temple every morning on his way to the office. He is initiated into the lesson of humility and feels that the only sustaining basis for action is to be use to others, "without vanity and without expectations and also without cleverness" (p. 143). He tells the young man who has come to join the Republic Day parade to consider him an apprentice and thinks that there is nothing wrong to have a second start:

> Consider me an apprentice and you will perhaps understand. Each morning, before I go to work, I come here. I sit on the steps of the temple and while they pray I wipe the shoes of the congregation. Then when they are gone...I stand at the doorstep and fold my hands smelling of leather and I say things. Be good, I tell myself. Be good. Be decent. Be of use. Then I beg forgiveness. Of a large host: my father, my mother, the Brigadier, the unknown dead of the war, of those whom I harmed... (pp. 142-143).

Ratan's inquisitiveness for puzzling questions of life is partly satisfied when Himmat Singh diagnoses the malady—the crookedness of Indian society and its cure as well:

> But if it was God's darkness, he asked, what was the cure? What was the cure of a crooked world. None, perhaps, Revolution, perhaps. Or perhaps—perhaps—he seemed to hesitate for a long time—perhaps God Himself. God alone perhaps could remove His darkness.
>
> But where was God, he cried out again, suddenly excited, his voice ringing with despair. What was God? And where? (pp. 145-146).

Standing the doorstep Ratan hopes that the young people can turn the tide though the future of the country looks gloomy. The dilemma about God adds another existential aspect to Ratan's existence. The words of Himmat Singh goad to view his existence from a new angle. He further tells Ratan: "My soul was killed, you put yours to pawn. But souls that were pawned could perhaps be retrieved" (p. 146). Ratan decides to retrieve his pawned soul by putting himself to use in spiritual humility and resignation to the Will of God. It is here that Joshi presents a contrast to other existential writers like Graham Greene. For Joshi, "the experience of the Absurd constitutes the starting point of his movement towards affirmation," and for Greene, "it is descent into abysmal pessimism" (Das: 45). In this way in *The Apprentice* Joshi suggests a different remedy to life's problems which is within the reach of common man. Ratan realizes that life may well be zero but it is not necessarily purposeless. He reaches his affirmation in his apprenticeship, wiping the shoes of the congregation in front of the temple. He remembers what his father had told him, "whatever, you do touches someone somewhere" (p. 143). However petrified and frozen our society may be, there is hope that if man is disposed to learn, as Ratan Rathor does, he may learn in no time and the novel ends with a dawn which is symbolic of man's regeneration: "But no matter. A dawn after all, is a dawn" (p. 144).

The way which Ratan chooses for the purification of his soul meets the vision of *Bhakti* in *The Bhagvadgita*: Ratan undergoes expiation and believes that purification is to be obtained not by any ritual, or dogma but by making amends. The polishing of shoes of the devotees by him cleanses the filth enveloping his soul. His earlier atheistic attitude towards life is gone and Ratan comes to believe that only God can help him. His sitting in front of a temple signifies his devotion (*Bhakti*) in which the devotee can appease his God just by praying to him meekly as Joshi suggests, "A stage comes in your evolution when you can do without rules, but you must have a tremendous self control...there is a long journey before you can reach that stage so that only few people are inclined to do that. There will be a time again when people will turn towards the divine and want to become instrument of God, rather than living for themselves" (Piciucco: 93). *The Bhagvadgita* on the other hand recommends humility as the first need for a devotee, "The devotee has a sense of utter humility. In the presence of the Ideal, he feels that he is nothing. God loves meekness, the utter prostration of the self"

(Radhakrishnan: 61). Ratan's existential decision to recover the lost self through an act of penitence reveals "the need to realise and prize one's integrity" (Reddy: 229).

The Apprentice shows a similarity to Albert Camus's *The Fall* in respect of its exposure of Ratan's hypocrisy. Like Baptiste Clamence he looks into his own deceptions, snobbery and corruption in a mocking way. In retrospect, he looks at his own fall and finds that he had willingly allowed himself to deteriorate and had no reason to find fault with the world. Earlier, he had been a victim of self-deception in which he holds himself innocent and blames others for his misdoings. Like Clamence, Ratan discovers that there can be no playing truant with life and there is no salvation outside it and he takes the responsibility on his own to affirm the meaning of life.

The laconic title of the novel *The Apprentice* hammers on the consciousness of the reader the very burden of the narrative powerfully. It implies that for leading a purposeful life in this world one has to undergo some sort of training to broadly acquaint oneself with its parameters. An inexperienced fresher ignorant of the ways of the world is destined to feel frustrated and tired of his existence. It is not without significance that the title word 'apprentice' appears on the penultimate page of the novel as if it conveys the very message of the work. While explaining its implications the protagonist adopts an exhorting tone:

> What am I apprenticed to? If I only exactly knew! Or if I could put into words what I do know. But life runs on approximations and if an approximation will do, you could say that I am learning to be of use. I know it is late in the day. But one must try and not lose heart, not yield, at any cost, to despair (p. 143).

The realisation—'life runs on approximations'—that dawns upon the protagonist is a veritable treasure of human experience. His confession that "I am learning to be of use" sums up the very essence of human life. Humility is a first step towards devotion (*Bhakti*) and by deciding to take up this unpleasant job at the temple doorstep Ratan Rathor initiates himself in the process of redemption through devotion. Joshi is not unmindful of the unbelievers in God and the next novel *The Last Labyrinth* grapples with this dimension of human situation.

WORKS CITED

Barret, William. *Irrational Man: A Study in Existential Philosophy*. London: Mercury Books, 1960.

Camus, Albert. *The Fall*. Harmondsworth: Penguin Books, 1968.

Das, R.J. "Moral Dilemma in Arun Joshi's *The Apprentice*," *Journal of Literature and Aesthetics*. 1, 2 (March 1981).

Joshi, Arun. *The Apprentice*. New Delhi: Orient Paperbacks, 1974; rptd. 1993. All further citations refer to this edition followed by paginations.

Mathai, Sujata. "I'm a Stranger to My Books," *The Times of India* (Bombay), 10 July (1984), 8.

Mathur, O.P. & Rai, G. "Arun Joshi and the Labyrinth of Life," R.K. Dhawan (ed). *The Fictional World of Arun Joshi*. New Delhi: Classical Publishing Co., 1971.

Piciucco, Pier Paolo. "An Interview with Arun Joshi," *Journal of Indian Writing in English*. 25, 1-2 (1997), 87-95.

Prasad, Hari Mohan. *Arun Joshi*. New Delhi: Arnold-Heinemann, 1985.

Radhakrishnan, S. (ed. & tr.). *The Bhagavadgita*. New Delhi: Harper Collins Publishers, 1993; rptd. 2000.

Reddy, V. Gopal. "*The Apprentice*: An Existential Study," R.K. Dhawan (ed.), *The Fictional World of Arun Joshi*.

Thakur, Guruprasad. "The Lost Lonely Questers in Arun Joshi's Fiction," R.K. Dhawan (ed.), *The Fictional World of Arun Joshi*.

5

DILEMMA OF A DOUBTING THOMAS: *THE LAST LABYRINTH*

Arun Joshi's fourth novel, *The Last Labyrinth* (1981) is a continuation of the existential quest dealt with in his earlier novels. Commonly regarded as his *magnum opus*, *The Last Labyrinth* won for its creator the prestigious Sahitya Akademi Award in1982. It explores the dilemma of existence in the life of Som Bhaskar, a millionaire industrialist and his incessant urge to understand the labyrinth of life.

The novelist conceives the world as *Maya* (a Labyrinth) where Man has to find his way to *moksha* (liberation) through *dharma* (duty), *artha* (wealth), and *kama* (desire). This is not possible until man follows the path shown by the philosophy of *karmayoga* in *The Bhagavadgita.* The thought of *karmayoga* shows that by the suppression of *kama* (desire), *krodha* (anger), *mada* (pride), *lobha* (greed), and *moha* (allurement) man can attain salvation. Man's failure to control these weaknesses paves the way of human suffering. The absurdity of his existence frightens man and he finds himself in a labyrinth. All this is due to the ignorance of his innate potentialities. He gets confused and believes that "being" is "having." This swells his pride and he wastes his energies without properly appreciating human existence, and is led to doubt even the existence of God. To avoid this, we must control the senses and "possess the faith with which no intellectual doubts disturb" (Radhakrishnan: 52). To 'Know Thyself' is the supreme vision of the *Vedanta.* This realisation of Eternal Self takes man to *moksha* (release) from the perplexities of this world. Arun Joshi while dealing with the

Hungers of the body, Hunger of the Spirit (Joshi, 1981: 11) has taken recourse to the Hindu philosophical thoughts. Commenting upon the thrust of his earlier novels, Joshi observed in precise terms:

> The first three, to me seem concerned generally about questions of identity and, probably ethics. The protagonists feel truncated, unfulfilled in some way. There is a withdrawal from the world, then a return to it, the process making them somehow more whole (Joshi, 1982: 5).

The Last Labyrinth also follows the pattern of "Truncation," "Withdrawal" and "Return" in the life of its protagonist, Som Bhaskar who passes from ignorance and its resultant agony to affirmation which however seems at times far-fetched. Like *The Foreigner, The Last Labyrinth* is written from the protagonist-narrator point of view. Som Bhaskar, a millionaire industrialist tells us in flashback the events involving him and another man's woman named Anuradha after whom he lusts and risks his business and life as well. Like the heroes of *The Foreigner* and *The Strange Case,* Som Bhaskar belongs to the upper society and adds a new perspective to the circumstances confronting the contemporary man.

When the novel opens we are acquainted with Som Bhaskar, the protagonist of the novel who becomes a millionaire at the age of 25 after his father's death. Though married to a woman of his choice who has borne him two children, he is hardly satisfied with his affluent position. Against the confusions, anxieties and agonies of his life emerges the metaphysical background of the novel. Som remembers his meeting with some Bhikkus at Madurai and says: "They only talked of Nirvana and that other visitor, the Royal Bhikku, Mahinda, Asoka's messenger, and how when he spoke in King Tissa's court the Emperor wept" (p. 9). Further metaphysical colour is added when we learn about Som's reaction after watching the board beside a monument which read: "There are beings who perish through not knowing the Dhamma...Go ye forth, O Bhikkus, and proclaim the Dhamma. There will be some who will understand...." (p. 9).

The Last Labyrinth obviously demonstrates the novelist's interest in metaphysical theories. Som's sleep routine informs us of his illness:

> Three to ten in the morning and four to six in the afternoon. There is nothing that K has not tried. Sleeping pills, tranquillisers, warm baths, But three to ten it remains and four to six. He is puzzled. I can see that. Your blood is only chemicals now, he says, pure unmanageable chemicals. Your body is God's chariot, says Tuka Ram. There you are! (p. 10).

We find him puzzled and ill to the extent that all the efforts of his family doctor K (Dr. Kashyap) have failed to bring about any change in his life. The mysterious voices that continually haunt him: "I want. I want. I want" describe his agony. Sent by his father to the world's finest universities for education, Som is among the big business magnetes of Bombay. His father, who was a scientist and a believer in metaphysical theories, has exerted a good impact over Som. Though Som is a product of reason, he frequently wants to discuss philosophy with others. He has realised somehow that material possessions are the ultimate goal of man, but his knowledge doesn't change him. At heart he is a mixture of contrary elements—'belief' and 'reason.' Som tells about the problem facing him:

> I knew of Krishna, of the lines he had spoken; of Buddha at Sarnath, under the full moon of July, setting in motion the wheel of Righteousness; of Pascal, on whom I did a paper at Harvard: 'Let us weigh the gain and loss in wagering that God is, let us estimate these two chances. If you gain, you gain all, if you lose, you lose nothing'. All this I knew and much else. And yet, at the age of thirty five, I could do no better than produce the same rusty cry: I want. I want (pp. 11-12).

Som Bhaskar represents the western-educated twentieth-century man who is experiencing the boredom and meaninglessness of his skeptical existence: "At thirty five, I was a worn out weary man incapable of spontaneous feeling" (p. 14). When he once looked at himself in the mirror he says: "lean, crowfooted, greying...I could not, then see the hunger but there was the boredom and the fed-up-ness, endless depths of it" (p. 21). Due to all this, he wakes in the middle of night, depressed and upset frequently. To keep this boredom at bay, he wants to be preoccupied with people, in drinking, and chit chat.

The other side of his personality is that Som has a deep desire to know everything in life. The outcome of man's belief in God as well as the existence of God dominate his speculations. Som is a product of Western Education so he can not believe anything that cannot be logically proved and herein lies his tragedy. His wife Geeta presents a sharp contrast to him since she is fully satisfied with her belief in God and also her life and his mother is also a lady of religious convictions. When Som once suggests her that she wouldn't get well at home she replies, "I will. Just wait and see," because she has a deep faith in Krishna. For Som, his mother's death proves to be a turning point. What angers him is the way his mother keeps on waiting for Krishna to cure her and flushes her tablets down the toilet. He thinks of her conduct as sheer foolishness. He looks at this whole event as a proof of God's unconcern towards human beings. From his mother's death onwards, he is never able to save himself from being a sceptic.

Som Bhaskar, like Sindi Oberoi, seems to be a product of two cultures. Born and brought up in India by his religious mother, he imbibes interest in religious faith and spiritual ethos. On the other hand, he has studied abroad as well and the western outlook has contributed a lot to his personality. His reliance on reason, materialistic outlook and practical wisdom are his acquisitions from the West. He has inherited a scientific attitude from his father and thus the two contrary things—science and religion—create a strain within his self and torture him. The opposite impulses of reason and intuition, illusion and reality, doubt and faith make him a psychological case. From his grandfather he inherits his fondness for woman and drink and runs after several women and has so many fornifications. But tragically enough, instead of having a sense of fulfilment, he has a deep sense of emptiness, of voids within and without: "It is the voids of the world, more than its objects, that bother me. The voids and the empty spaces, within and without" (p. 47).

In order to find a release from his anguish, he searches for something other than God which can satisfy him. Som becomes a battleground of contrary things: "Hunger of the body. Hunger of the spirit. You suffer from one or the other, or both" (p. 11) signifies his confused character. In this battle between contraries his mind sides with body. In an effort to keep himself preoccupied with something or the other, he goes to Benares to deal with Aftab Rai, a plastic manufacturer who had invited him to come to city. Aftab Rai presents himself as a man of culture and refinement with oriental leaning. His talks with Som often tend to be philosophical. Aftab's ancestors were the rulers of Lucknow who were forced to flee to Rohilkhand, Nepal and Benares after the seige of Imambara by the British. Now Aftab lives in an ancient mansion named Lal Haveli built by his ancestors in Benares and now owns a plastic manufacturing company. Though Aftab is not good at handling the business he has finer understanding of life than Som Bhaskar.

When Som enters the mysterious Lal Haveli, he meets Anuradha, an antique looking woman and feels attracted by her beauty. She is like "a monument: tall, handsome, ruined...thirty, thirtyfive...from Bengal, from Sikkim, from the valleys of Nepal" (p. 12). This is the only information which Som gets at Lal Haveli. He at once feels as if Anuradha is indispensable for him. The mysterious Lal Haveli in which Anuradha lives with her so-called husband (Aftab) without any formal marriage puzzles him much. Perhaps the entire haveli had been built as "a maze" (p. 34). It is from this Lal Haveli that Anuradha starts to dominate Som's thoughts and passions. He is fascinated by her charm, "she was not self-conscious about her body of whose grace and sensuousness she seemed unaware" (p. 41). The successive pages of the novel, mainly the first part, unfold Som's indomitable hunger for sex. Blind by passion he wants to possess her again and again. His excessive infatuation with Anuradha makes him a casanova as Leela Sabnis, a professor calls him a "compulsive fornicator" (p. 80). Though Som has gone to deal with Aftab's Company, Anuradha exercises such an overpowering fascination over him that he neglects his business, his family and his health in an effort to win her.

Though a typical product of deprivation and suffering Anuradha has perception of life whereas Som is devoid of it. She has profound faith in God and Som accepts that she is a woman "gifted with a special vision, a vantage point high above the earth, from where she could see the melee below as ordinary men could not: And it was as though the vision always left her sadder, taking away from her the hope and the laughter with which she had been born" (p. 58). She had faced many an upheaval in life. She is an illegitimate child born of an insane mother who earned her living by singing to strangers. Her mother was taken away by one of her lovers who killed her with a broken whisky bottle. Anuradha's aunt brought her up and managed her modest education. In her effort to become a film actress, she was seduced by many producers. At present she is living with Aftab without any formal marriage. She says: "You can't marry every one you love. So, why marry any one at all?" (p. 43) When Som asks about her marriage with Aftab and if she would like to marry someone, she says: "I can imagine I am married to Aftab. I can imagine I am married to you. My mother used to imagine she was married to Krishna" (p. 128). Here Anuradha puts a contrast to Som who is prone to look for reasons and surety of things. Her faith in God inherited from the Vaishnavite mother puzzles Som most.

Lal Haveli is the central metaphor of the novel. It symbolises all those questions which keep Som tormenting. It symbolises human life, death and the understanding of God. Som comments: "I realized, that it was a maze that we were moving through. Perhaps, the entire Haveli has been built as a maze" (p. 35). Som's visit to several places with Aftab and Anuradha gives us an insight into Som's psyche. When he goes to Manikarnika Ghat, the burning place, he becomes afraid of the thought of his death:

> At twenty two I had patronized my father. Ten years later, at the hour nearing mid-night, the sight of all those funeral pyres on the Manikarnika Ghat, the smell of burning flesh and burstling of bones, gave me one big shaking down

> before I got hold of myself. The flames, lighting this, hiding that, throwing crazy shadows all over made matters worse (p. 45).

From Manikarnika Ghat, Aftab and Anuradha take Som to the other bank of Ganga where he meets Gargi, an ascetic woman of about forty. She is deaf and mute but communicates by writing on her pad. After meeting Gargi Som experiences unusual change in him: "I felt as though it was not Ganga but some unknown stream, in some unknown segment of the universe, leading to a reality that I had not known" (p. 49). Though he realises this change entering in his personality, he ignores it as a part of his hallucinations at this point. He enquires about Gargi and Anuradha tells him her whereabouts. Gargi's father was a prince who later turned a Sufi, a pir and lived with Aftab's father and blessed his son with eyesight. Som doubts Sufi's competence and Anuradha remarks: "You are wrong about many things. You are wrong even about yourself. You think you know a lot, when, in fact you don't" (p. 61). She senses Som Bhaskar's plight as one destitute of faith: "I know you want something. You badly want something. I could see that the first time we met. But it is not me. That too, I can see. I told you so in the dargah" (pp. 58-59).

The relationship between Som and Anuradha is one of the most complex relationships in the novel. She gradually acquires centre stage in his life. Though he returns to Bombay after Anuradha rebukes him, he repeatedly goes to Benares to meet her. Lal Haveli attracts him in some mysterious ways. Anuradha becomes a labyrinth herself and Som expects a transparency from her:

> There was a mystery about Anuradha that I had yet to crack. She should have been no more to me than a woman trying to save her lover's (husband's?) property. She should have been transparent. Why should she appear mysterious unless, possibly, there was a mystery within me that, in her proximity got somehow stirred, as one tuning fork might stir another (p. 89).

In Bombay, Som fails to save himself from frustration. His

gentle wife Geeta knows about Som's affair with Anuradha but she is calm and loyal to Som. Som accepts that his weakness lies in his pride and distrust in the mechanisms of the world: "But I needed the trust—who doesn't? I needed it all the more because I did not trust myself, or my men, or my fate, or the ceaseless travel on the social wheel...what I needed most was to be reassured that all was well" (p. 63). His sceptic temperament coupled with his arrogance multiplies his problems. One marks his intemperate behaviour when he gets infuriated at the slight delay in meeting with Mrs. Bedi, the social worker, he has to oblige with donation:

> Why couldn't they make her stand in the front? Twenty five thousand rupees are so chickenfeed. I gave her two minutes to show up. Two minutes or I would go. I had better things to do (p. 64).

When he finally hands over the cheque to Mrs. Bedi, she does not even look at the amount mentioned, but folds her hands out of gratitude. Geeta's presence among those social workers startles him further. He sees her standing in front of the stalls of dolls, holding a brown teddy bear having a badge on her shoulder. She appears to him as the perfect emblem of endurance as opposed to his restive disposition. Som's problems are further increased by an oncoming melancholia. He remembers his illness before his marriage when he had thought that he would overcome it by his money and fame:

> Melancholia! For God's sake! I couldn't imagine a more ridiculous, foolish, humiliating death. I would fight it to the bitter end. And to fight I would have all the equipment. Money I already had. I shall have a wife and children and fame. Yes, fame too. What could be a better antidote to melancholia than fame! (p. 72).

Som had thought of leading a happy life with his children and wife but they have dwindled into insignificance for him so much so that he doesn't even mention them in his story. His consultations with psychiatrist do not help him to forget his nagging fear of death. He is suggested by one psychiatrist that his restlessness would cease if he meets his soul mate. Though he attaches no significance to the recommendations of psychiatrist he goes to meet Dr. Leela Sabnis with whom Som has an old acquaintance.

Som's meeting with Dr. Leela Sabnis, a Michigan educated lady gives a thrust to the theories of various philosophers and thinkers like Freud, Descartes and Spinoza. For him she symbolises western culture. Though a scholar, she is proud of having been divorced by her husband for her love of books and also of leading a free life. Som calls her a 'mechanic of the spirit' but she turns out to be of totally incapable of giving him the answers he has been looking for. In spite of all her reading of Freud and American and European philosophers, she is as confused as Som. She prescribes the help of Cartesian philosophy to Som and says: "It is Descartes you need to understand" (p. 79). She finds the cause of Som's problems in his separation of matter from spirit. Som doesn't find any clue from her discussions about his illusions. To Som, she is a muddled creature:

> Leela Sabnis was a muddled creature. As muddled as me. Muddled by her ancestry, by marriage, by divorce, by too many books... Her first words would be "Let me begin where I left off," reeling off diagnoses, half sense, half poppycock, too much analysis (p. 78).

Their discussion of Spinoza's rejection of the Cartesian duality of matter and spirit and his philosophy that "both matter and spirit embraced in God, and flowed from him" (p. 81) proves distasteful to Som. All talk of intuition and soul proves to be a wild goose chase and while leaving her, he realises that Leela has only provided sexual enjoyment for some days. On the spiritual level, his understanding is zero:

> In the world of matter we had fed on sex and now we were satiated. In the world of the spirit we still enjoyed conversation. The two worlds, by her lights, did not meet, could not meet.... May be, that was why we fell apart. What I needed, perhaps, was something, somebody, somewhere in which the two worlds combined (pp. 81-82).

Though Leela Sabnis embodies the Descartean principle, "I

think therefore I am" (p. 80) and asserts that everything as well as God and soul can be reasoned through but Som is not endowed with that kind of confidence as she has. He gets again tormented by the memories of Anuradha and her city. However to get rid of her obsession he goes on a tour to Europe with his wife but Anuradha's memories haunt him everywhere. On his return to Bombay, he plans a trip to Benares to meet her.

Som's wreckless search to get someone in whom the two worlds of matter and spirit combined seems to reach its consummation in Anuradha. She is the only person who gives him a release from his anxieties and illusions. Som as a sceptic cannot realise this by himself. At this point, the role of Gargi, the deaf-mute daughter of a Sufi pir becomes of paramount importance. Som goes to Gargi and seeks her advice. She writes on her pad, "God will send someone to help you... Someone who has known suffering" (p. 118). Her indication is clearly towards Anuradha as she further communicates: "Don't quarrel. She is your *shakti*" (p. 121). By employing the word *shakti*, Gargi means the divine power which can transform Som's craving for sex into his sublimation for the realisation of spirit. However, Som regards Anuradha's love a purging experience and finds himself instinctively drawn to Lal Haveli again and again: "I was fated to return to that haveli over and over. We possessed each other with singular ferocity, neither willing to loosen her clasp" (p. 121).

One day while Som is in the stupor of whisky, Anuradha advises him to visit the shrine of Krishna in the mountains in order to inculcate his belief in God. Som's involvement with Anuradha turns out to be the realization of the existence of God for him and the consequent liberation of the soul. At this point of the novel Som is still gripped by his obsessive existential questions. He goes to Gargi again and enquires her about human situation and asks her in an effort to mock at her:

> The point is that this spirit is there. And if it is there, if Man has inherited it, then what is he to do with it? In other words, what precisely is expected of him,...of everyone else? Darwin didn't say how we are supposed to evolve further (p. 132).

Som points to Gargi of the evolution of man from the Lizard called Hatteria as has been propounded by the scientists on the islands of New Zeland with a third eye, like *Shiva*, about a hundred million years ago. This is a proof of his reasoning aptitude as he further elaborates: "Nothing had interested me more than the secrets of the universe. Blessed little good, all that curiosity had done me" (p. 129).

Though the elusive experiences of Som's life force him to believe in the presence of God to some extent, his defiance comes in his way intermittently. On a visit to a temple on *janmastami*, Anuradha calls him into the temple, but he refuses: "I am not coming... Too crowded for my taste" (p. 130). He is too arrogant to accept God as an entity in the temple. When Gargi, Aftab and Anuradha join again, he gives them a dose of the Darwin's theory of evolution and also tells them of the presence of spirit in the long skulled, short faced men found in Cro-Magnon cave in France. When Aftab suggests that man must have visions to understand the spirit, Som scoffs at it and says that visions are dime a dozen. Anuradha explicates it further: "May be Krishna begins where Darwin left off" (p. 132). Som's disbelief and disgust get further multiplied when Som and Anuradha walk through the ghats of Benares. People are celebrating the birthday of Krishna. The chanting of *Hare Krishna*, the *aartis*, and the sound of drums vibrate the air. Som thinks of all these as mere humbug and the city of Benares as 'the city of perversions' whereas Anuradha goes muttering prayers and making offerings at every shrine.

After some days Som returns to Bombay to undergo a lot of elusive experiences which he cannot reason himself. He suffers a massive heart attack and on recovering to some extent, he contacts Anuradha who expresses her inability to see him any more. Som's ego is hurt at Anuradha's indifference. He wants to possess her entirely: "I wanted her body and soul, every bit of her. I was not willing to share a hair of her body with any one" (p. 133). He decides to ruin Aftab's business and thus to teach Anuradha a lesson. He advises his business manager Mr. Thapar to buy Aftab's shares. Som's panic is the result of Anuradha's unexpected refusal to him. This fear sets a chain reaction and they extend upto 'elevators, bridges, motor cars, sea breeze, electric switches and canned food' (p. 152). Som even resolves to settle his scores with Anuradha with his grandfather's revolver kept hidden in the rosewood cabinet. His emotional and mental condition show us his agony in the labyrinth of his life. He can only think of death in the last labyrinth. The recurrent dreams which he undergoes in night suggest a lot about his truncated state. The unquenched desires torment him and he dreams of flying high in a plane towards a mountain glowing in brightness with Aftab as co-pilot:

> I am flying towards a mountain. Mountain with a snow-covered peak. The plane is one of those yellow trainers you see at the flying club. I am in the front. Someone else in the back. I cannot make out who it is. The person in the back has all the gears of pilots and I cannot really see much of him. We fly through clouds and mist.... The sky above is black as pitch.... Even though the sky is black and there is no sun, the mountain glows. From within as it were. All of a sudden there is more mist and fog and rain. Sheets of glassy rain. I ask the man behind where the wipers are. The man laughs (p. 159).

This dream of Som is very suggestive as it clarifies his unconscious efforts to discover the ultimate reality which is the glowing mountain full of divine light. This light is the light of self-knowledge for which his soul has been craving since long. The mist, cloud and the darkness of the sky represent the illusory nature of Som's life. The pilot who is driving him towards reality represents Aftab, Anuradha and Gargi who are the agents to lead him to his self-realization. Unless and until he bids farewell to his lust, anger, pride, greed and hatred, the goal of liberation will remain illusive for him.

The illusory nature of Som's psyche is further observed when Aftab and Som meet in the hotel. Som's detectives are seriously searching for Anuradha's missing shares. While they play chess, they discuss about belief in God. He tells Som that belief in God is like having a third king in a game of chess. Aftab advises him to give up questioning God's existence:

> You have to sacrifice before you are given. You can't have your cake and eat it, too...you want to have faith. But you also want to reserve the right to challenge your own faith when it suits you (p. 166).

Since this counsel is not to his taste, Som humiliates Aftab for his inefficiency to handle his business. Aftab gives him a gift from Anuradha, a silver image of Krishna playing the flute. The irony of the situation is that Som's detectives find out that Anuradha's shares are with 'Krishna' and they are kept in the custody of the Secretary of the temple. He insists to go up to mountains to meet Krishna by himself in spite of K's warnings: "He is going to die climbing those mountains looking for those shares" (p. 172). Som remains adamant and undertakes the arduous journey to the temple of Krishna.

It is worth noting that Som gets prepared to meet Krishna by himself. On his way to temple he learns from his doctor that Anuradha has given him up in order to save Som from death and some miracle has happened which has saved him. Som treats it as another labyrinth for him as the existence of Krishna. For him Krishna is a complex labyrinth to understand:

> No, there was nothing simple about this thing. There was nothing simple about Krishna. Had it been so, He would not have survived ten thousand years. He would have died along with the gods of the Pharaohs, the Sumerians, the Incas. Krishna was about as simple as the labyrinths of Aftab's Haveli (p. 173).

At night Som dreams that his plane is going to crash into a fiery mountain. This dream is symbolical of his confrontation with Krishna and with Krishna lies his self-affirmation. He reminds himself of the Cartesian dictum '*Cogito ergo sum*' and his point of view takes a turn. He thinks that: "Surely, if he could hold shares, He could give other evidence of His existence" (p. 179).

The other events of Som's journey to the hills increase his confidence and lessen his fear of death to a considerable extent. He meets a young boy wearing a yellow pullover and corduroy cap. The boy's confidence and interest in his effort to find a special kind of pebble having a star in its centre amazes Som.

His positive attitude to journey notwithstanding its result presents a sharp contrast to Som's behaviour after his failure to possess Anuradha. The boy has come with his ailing grandfather who wishes to die near the mountain shrine. Som mocks at this foolishness but he realises that death is inevitable and one should not fear it. This meeting with the old man enlightens Som considerably. The boy's presence at his grandfather's funeral boosts Som's courage to face death and he says:

> I wandered what we were doing there, what I was doing there, I who had always avoided funerals. I marvelled at the boy's wondrous equanimity. He watched the proceedings through large alert eyes, as it was a play and not a real funeral. Did he realise that this was Death? For that matter, did I? May be that was where the trick lay. Along with the old man we had travelled to the other world, chanting, free from fear. You might as well be afraid of a train travelling from one station to another. That black lake, those bronze cliffs, were certainly another station (p. 194).

To the little boy, his grandfather and the lepers who are in their way to the mountain shrine, this uphill journey is a matter of faith in God. This faith strengthens them to face death and their failures in life whereas Som finds him completely broken in these situations. He reaches the mountain shrine and meets Gargi there. He is surprised when K tells Som how Anuradha pleaded Gargi to know that Som is dying of heart attack. He observes:

> Anuradha persisted, wept, begged and threatened. She said to you she could not live without Som and she would eat poison if something happened to him. She said your father had given Aftab his eyesight so why could you not save Som's life. She said she would not go home until you did something for Som (p. 205).

K further tells Som how Anuradha got the assurance of Gargi's help by promising that she would leave Som for good. K asks Gargi:

> I am a medical doctor. I do not believe in things in which Anuradha believes. But I know for a fact that Som had no chance whatsoever and I want to know. Did you save him? Anuradha says you did. And in return for what you did, she says, you made her promise that she would give up Som forever. That to her, Som would be dead, either way. Is this true? Please tell me (p. 206).

Som thinks that K's story is a concocted one and he is not ready to believe it so easily. Gargi tells him that Anuradha had given her jewels and shares as a thanksgiving for his recovery. The package of shares are with the Secretary of the temple. Som's disbelief in all this mumbo-jumbo does not end even at this point. His confusion persists and he questions himself whether his quest has ended:

> Was this is, then? The terminus? The last of the labyrinth? A tobacco-stained house; a register with my father's signature; a temple on a hill; flags in the wind; a deaf mute priestess; hints of a miracle? Was it this that I had wanted all my life? Was this the answer to the relentless chant "I want, I want." Why was it so unsatisfying? Or, may be, the labyrinth hadn't ended. Something else lay ahead, something more fundamental than a miracle, something I would know only if I took those shares from Gargi. If God existed, if a miracle had taken place, and now if I now walked off with the shares—and with Anuradha—I should perhaps die (p. 211).

In spite of this short introspection, Som is determined not to leave Anuradha. He tells Gargi: "I cannot give up Anuradha, you know that. In the absence of evidence I intend to challenge the whole thing: I want to take not only these shares but also Anuradha. It scares me but I have no choice" (p. 213).

Som's arrogance, pride and ignorance muddle his mind again and again. He has a touch of defiance which has made him a doubting Thomas forever. Gargi's response to his arrogant remark is thought-provoking: "God does not work in this simple manner. God does not seek revenge. Man's *ahankara* brings him revenge enough" (pp. 213-214). Gargi advises Som to renounce his pride and selfishness and to accept God as the saviour of mankind. Only a belief in God can give man solace from confusion in this materialistic scenario. She repeats: "There is no harm in believing that God exists" (p. 213). Gargi reminds him of the vastness of the Cosmos which is the work of God and it is not easy to understand God in such a small period: "We are all children trying to reach up to a crack in the door to peep into a room" (p. 214).

After all these revelations by Gargi, Som feels that he was at mistake and he must mend his ways for a full realisation of the essence of life. He is completely disarmed after his meeting with Gargi:

> I lay down by the stream, the bundle under my head. Above me, the vast canopy of the sky suddenly appeared as though I had never seen it before. I was reminded of Prince Andrew, knocked down like a dummy without firing a shot. He had imagined himself to be ambitious...lying in the mud, cannon balls flying over him, he had stared at the vast cosmic impersonal dome of the sky and wondered: My God, where have I been all these years. Why had I never looked at the sky before (pp. 215-216).

Much of Som's affirmation is brought about by his last visit to Benares and his meeting with Aftab and Anuradha. When Som reaches there, Aftab tries to persuade him to leave them alone and mocks at his pride and adds: "You don't understand us. You work by logic. By your brain. You are proud of your education or what you consider education. There is only an understanding that only suffering and humiliation bring. Anuradha has that. Even I have a bit of it. You are empty of that understanding" (p. 217). Still Som is determined to meet Anuradha who refuses to accompany him to Bombay. She warns him to go away as soon as possible from Lal Haveli as there is danger to his life: "You don't understand. You don't know these people. Things could happen to you in this Haveli and no one would ever know" (p. 219).

The next morning Som finds Anuradha missing from the Haveli. He comes to Bombay in a desolate mood and starts to mend his ways. He thinks that God shall excuse him for all his sins and arrogance. He pleads to Anuradha in his thoughts:

> Anuradha, listen. Listen to me wherever you are. Is there God where you are? Have you met him? Does He have a face? Does He speak? Does He hear? Does He understand the language that we speak? Anuradha, if there is a God and if you have met Him and if He is willing to listen, then, Anuradha, my soul, tell Him, tell this God to have mercy upon me. Tell Him, I am weary...He will listen to you (p. 223).

At this juncture of the novel, we are given an indication of Som's spiritual affirmation and one hopes that he will remain steadfast in future. Anuradha is the only *shakti* (means) who can transform Som's "hunger of the body" into "hunger of the spirit" but Som's realisation can be worked out by Som only: "One had probably to rise up to the crack by oneself" (p. 215). Towards the close of the novel, the last labyrinth becomes a realisation of the existence of God or the death of the body. This understanding might lead him to the consequent liberation (affirmation) of the soul. In this whole process of affirmation from ignorance in the darkness of *maya* to the light in *moksha,* the novelist emphasises the philosophy of *karmayoga* of *The Bhagavadgita*. This philosophy is quite different from the philosophy of *Sanyasa* which is the abandonment of worldly affairs and actions after self-realisation as Gautam Buddha did. *Karmayoga* does not propose to abandon worldly affairs but it suggests "to perform them in such a way that they do not create any difficulty in the matter of obtaining release" (Tilak: 82).

The title of the novel seems to be highly significant as it represents a great mystery that lies in the novel. On the surface level, it refers to the last of labyrinths in Lal Haveli at Benares, like the historical Bhulbhulaiyan at Lucknow. Lal Haveli which is the centre of the actions in the novel is situated amid the tortuous lanes of Benares. It refers to a puzzling structure, a sort of *chakravyuha,* constructed to mainly mislead an army so that it fails to come out of it. In order to baffle the enemies, the haveli is built like a labyrinth with rooms within rooms, and with corridors that only bring the person back to square one. On the metaphorical level, Som Bhaskar's world is as confusing and illusive as the location of Lal Haveli itself and its baffling labyrinths. Arun Joshi has used the word labyrinth in similar sense in his earlier novels as well. Sindi Oberoi in *The Foreigner* talks of his sad affairs with Kathy as the wound that still bled "somewhere in the labyrinth of my consciousness" (Joshi, 1968: 61). Similarly Billy Biswas in *The Strange Case* says that life's meaning lies "not in the glossy surfaces of our pretentions but in those dark mossy labyrinths of the soul that languish forever, hidden from the dazzling light of the sun" (Joshi, 1971: 4). A labyrinth has also been defined as "the complex prison built by Daedalus for king Minos to contain the Minotaur. The word is derived from *Labrys,* the sacred double axe of the Cretions and there was a temple of bull cult in Crete. This labyrinth was so complicated that none could escape once it was entered into.... The name was applied not only to building...but to all kind of mazes" (Funk and Wagnals: 598). To Som, the maroon blue room of Lal Haveli seems to be the last labyrinth and his own inability to free himself proves the prison like character of Lal Haveli. He becomes inseparable from its inhabitants and it is revealed symbolically when Som sees his own image in the portraits of the blue room:

> Turning a corner I was startled by an apparition. Careworn, holding a cigarette in one hand, it looked as though for many centuries it had lived in that bleak house. I stared breathless, realizing, suddenly that I was staring at my own image (p. 32).

The labyrinth of the haveli continues to puzzle and confuse Som and create in him a kind of void, and as a result he utters these words as a refrain: "I want. I want. I want" (p. 11). He is caught in the labyrinth and fails to carve his way out of it. His love for Anuradha, Leela Sabnis, and also for his wife Geeta and the short poise given by the mute Gargi place him in a psychic condition. Som's attainment of faith is difficult because in order to possess it, one has to make a complete surrender of oneself, one's selfishness and pride. In this way in *The Last Labyrinth,* Arun Joshi shows the predicament of the unbelievers. Som's agony is a result of his dilemmas eating into the very vitals of his religious conviction. This novel is a variation of the other novels of Arun Joshi. All other heroes progress from their anguished and alienated state to affirmation but the protagonist of *The Last Labyrinth* is an exception. In a letter to V. Gopal Reddy Arun Joshi wrote on 8th January, 1981:

> Alienation of my novels which I have written so far ultimately leads them back to community. I realized that in my latest novel *The Last Labyrinth* for the first time it does not happen (Reddy: 90).

The novel ends with Som making an attempt to suicide and Geeta restrains him from doing so "as though rousing a man from sleep" (p. 224).

The lives of Anuradha, Aftab, his father, Gargi and the theories proposed by Leela pose to Som Bhaskar as mazes in a labyrinth. The observation of Sujata Mathai is quite right when she says that Joshi "sees lives as labyrinths—hopeless mazes where you may get secrets of the core of life" (Mathai: 8).

Som's odyssey around the world proves as futile as the enemy's wanderings might have been in the labyrinths of Lal Haveli. He finds that his voyage to Europe and America with Geeta does not bring any consolation to his restive soul. Thus, the labyrinth stretches everywhere from Bombay and Benares, "to the Maya to Geeta, to the very edges of this beach" (p. 157). Later on he thinks Death to be the last labyrinth. He fears death whenever he becomes ill "both within and without" (p. 48), in the funeral pyres and in the burning flesh of Manikarnika Ghat. Further he dreams of being in a narrow alley on both sides of which stand deserted houses and at the end of it lies a shroud. He fails to recall and recognise it. Then he dreams that the alley "turned into the Blue Room with Aftab's ancestors smiling down" (p. 105) at him. He thinks that his life too shall be terminated soon. The Blue Room is also a part of the labyrinth of Lal Haveli. For Som Bhaskar his situation is so better than an ant's moving in a maze. His life and its activities are misdirected and he fails to reach a clear goal. The character of Anuradha puzzles Som and Aftab. Her disappearance in the last has no explanation. Their search for Anuradha is of no avail and both make their life agonised and miserable. This becomes clear from Aftab's letter to Som: "I can't live without her...endlessly I walk the mazes...night turns into day...day into night...I knock my head against the wall...cry out my love for her...she does not listen...I am finished" (p. 222). Thus, Anuradha's character adds to the mysterious character of the labyrinth in the novel.

It is crystal clear that Som's suffering is born out of his disbelief. He suffers from tension, disturbance, hysteria, neurosis and insomnia. The other people around him are happy even in their suffering on account of their qualitatively different attitude to life. He frequently discusses Kierkegaard and Descartes and remembers Kierkegaard saying: "Prayer does not change God but it changes him who prays" (p. 118). Som thus becomes a tortured soul and on him all forces of *Maya* are let loose. Leela Sabnis had described Descartes as a cure for his disease. This reference to Descartes is enough to give us the idea that the sceptic approach to God can leave human beings lost, tormented and alienated. Even when Som goes to join the celebrations on *Janmastami,* he is agitated by the memories of Anuradha's beautiful body: "I wasn't interested in Darwin or Krishna... All I wanted was her. I wanted her body and soul, every bit of her. I wasn't willing to share a hair of her body with any one" (p. 133). He thus becomes a perfect example of the people mentioned by Lord Krishna in the *Gita*: "Men who have no faith, not attaining to me...return to the path of mortal living" (Radhakrishnan: 238). Though he visits the shrine but he is tormented by anger because he fails to meet Anuradha. Som's reception of the shares of Anuradha unfold his greed. He argues with Gargi about the existence of God. To question God's existence is contrary to salvation and the Doubting Thomas is doomed to extinction (Radhakrishnan: 172). Man's affirmation lies upon himself. Though Som gives us some subtle hints as to mending his ways and become a devoted being for us he remains a disbeliever till the end of the novel.

The novel *The Last Labyrinth* has a religious background and it shows that affirmation is possible only by following the path of *dharma*. Only *dharma* can give man solace and poise amid the labyrinths of life. Man has only to establish a balance between three essential ingredients of life, action (*karma*), knowledge (*jnana*), and devotion (*bhakti*) to overcome the miseries of human situation. Of Joshi's protagonists, only Som remains lost because he reasons relentlessly to utmost limit. He has neither the intuition to become a believer nor he is sure that his reason can answer everything. A critic rightly regards Som as "an archetype of the new man and *The Last Labyrinth* is a fictional *tour-de-force* on the chaos of existence and the crisis of consciousness" (Prasad: 239). *The Last Labyrinth* thus expresses an existential concern which is basically a Hindu preoccupation derived from the *Vedas*, the *Upanishads* and *The Bhagavadgita*. Like modern Existentialists, the Hindu philosophers have considered the study of man's existence inseparable from the study of self itself. They have devoted themselves to the questions like the nature of man, the character of the world and the ways of man's upliftment through his affirmation. This can happen only through his spiritual inclinations which provide an insight into reality. Hindu scriptures conceive the world as a progressive manifestation of the Absolute. Man, by an understanding of his life, leads to the realisation of the Eternal Self and reaches his *moksha* from the labyrinth of this *sansara* (world).

It is not simply coincidental that the most ancient city of the World, Benares, is the central locale of the novel with Lal Haveli as its axis. When it comes to grappling with spiritual values Indian novelists in English invariably weave the structure of their plots in or around Benares and Raja Rao's *The Serpent And The Rope* is its best specimen. Its well known line—'All brides be Benares born'—underlines the preoccupation of the artist that the children born of such brides will inherit spiritual values from their very birth. Incidentally, Arun Joshi was born in Benares (as has been mentioned in the opening chapter) and he matured into a sensitive artist imbibing the spiritual ambience of this city situated on the trident of Lord Shiva, an altogether different world in the cosmos. No wonder that he uses words with heavily loaded religious connotations in *The Last Labyrinth*. Some of these with abundant frequency include *kirtans, prasad, aarti, nirvana, bhikkus, sadhus, tantrik, tantras, bhakti, shakti, panda, brahma, Rudra, Visnu, Krishna* and *Shiva*. The following excerpt testifies to Joshi's ability to render reality with the help of suggestiveness:

> Across the steps, in a staggered rows, half a dozen men, their marvellous oiled bodies faintly gleaming, barrelled through marathen of Calisthenics. A young Sanskrit scholar recited hymns at the top of his voice. I thought of my father and his little Book of the Upanishads. Another boy, equally young, corrected him. Did Panini ever live in Benares? Bebind the scholars, two young men drowned in *bhang*, did a fancy jig. Boatmen, jugglers, vagrants, monkey men, idlers, beggars, flutists, bathers, the watchers of funeral pyres, junkies, medicine men, vendors, each sat in his appointed place, as if on a stage, performing parts that they had performed over the millenia (p. 48).

The religion is a matter of conviction and the story of *The Last Labyrinth* demonstrates that the fate of sceptics is bound to be miserable and tormented. Despite undergoing spiritually fruitful experiences Som Bhaskar can not repose full faith in religious values as is manifest in his attempt to commit suicide. Had he been able to adopt an affirmative attitude to life, he would have certainly refrained from nursing such ideas. Since the novel is dedicated to Joshi's children—'Arjun, Nihar and Shonar'—it is possible to infer that he wishes his children to inculcate positive values in life. The last novel *The City and The River* to be taken up in the next chapter continues this quest for faith.

WORKS CITED

Funk and Wagnals. *Standard Dictionary of Folklore, Mythology and Legend*. New York: Harper and Row Publishers, 1984.

Joshi, Arun. *The Foreigner*. New Delhi: Hind Pocket Books, 1968; rptd. Orient Paperbacks, 1993.

——. *The Last Labyrinth*. New Delhi: Orient Paperbacks, 1981.

——. *News Letter*. Mysore: Indian Association for Commonwealth Literature and Language Studies. 10, 1 (Jan 1982), 5.

——. *The Strange Case of Billy Biswas*. New Delhi: Asia Publishing House, 1971.

Mathai, Sujata. "I'm a Stranger to My Books." *The Times of India*, Bombay. 10 July (1983), 8.

Prasad, Hari Mohan. *Arun Joshi*. New Delhi: Arnold-Heinemann, 1985.

Radhakrishnan, S. (ed. & tr.). *The Bhagavadgita*. New Delhi: Harper Collins Publishers, 1993.

Reddy, V. Gopal. "From Alienation to Community: A Note on the Novels of Arun Joshi," *Kakatia Journal of English Studies*. 7 (1985-86).

Tilak, Bal Gangadhar. *Srimad Bhagawadgita Rahasya* (tr.), B.S. Suktankar. Poona: Aryabhusan Press, 1965.

6

Vision of the Ultimate Truth: *The City and The River*

Arun Joshi's last novel *The City and The River* (1990) also centres around the basic principles of Hindu philosophy which teaches an affirmative attitude to life. The novel presents before us a city which is in the jaws of destruction due to its people who never seek the righteous way of living. Though the city dealt with is apparently contemporary, the issues which Joshi has raised are cosmic and philosophical. Throughout the novel, there is a conflict in the city folk to choose between the "allegiance to God" and "the allegiance to Man" or in other words between religion and politics. The city dwellers adopt a wrong path and face their doom. The river that flows by the side of the city represents Nature and it takes the shape of an irrepressible ocean and sweeps away the city. The doctrine of *Karma* asserts that man's final growth depends on him. His future is no pre-determined. He is a responsible agent who by the "integration of *Karma, Jnana* and *Bhakti*" (Rao: 150) reaches his salvation. If he chooses the opposite, he is bound to face his doom. In this way, the city dealt with in the novel is a collection of individuals who if taken together make their "own horoscope" by their actions. If the city is destroyed in the end, it is solely because of the wrong doings of its inhabitants. This novel has a clearcut message for its reader to uphold age-tested values of conviction and commitment.

Joshi has used various myths, legends and archetypes to suggest the value of an authentic life, faith and right action—the barest necessity of modern man. The novelist depicts the horror and terror unleashed on society when a handful of individuals like the Grand Master become ambitious and selfish. This political scenario of the city is used as backdrop of the novel which helps the novelist in presenting a contemporary problem with the metaphysical overview of creation and disintegration, *sristi* and *pralaya* dealt in Indian myths. Whenever human beings degenerate, anarchy and meaninglessness take them in their grip leading them nowhere. If they do not mend their ways the process of *sristi* and *pralaya* after a period of time is to go on unless the whole world is purified. The canvas of *The City and The River* is very vast and encompasses within its range time, God, Man and Nature.

The novel opens with a Prologue which relates the last day of the Nameless One with the Great Yogeshwara his teacher. The narrative framework of the novel is mythical and its narrational pattern reveals that it is a story told by an old wise teacher, a Guru, to his keen disciple preparing him to enter a new world after the complete destruction of an old city:

> "Do you hear music, my son?" asked the Great Yogeshwara.
> "Yes, father. And the dancing of a god."
> "That is good. I shall tell you now a tale and in my telling, perhaps you will know who you are. Listen, this is how it goes" (Joshi, 1990: 11).

Right from the start of the novel the reference to myths and archetypes is quite suggestive. The sound of the dance is the dance *tandava* of Lord Shiva who dances to bring '*pralaya*' in this world when it becomes sinful and corrupt. The conflict between the spirit and the body is also suggested in the Prologue:

> Both kinds of thought shall I teach you. I shall lead you to the grain and I shall lead you to the chaff. Keep the grain and the chaff apart, always, for much harm has come of their mixing (p. 10).

The Great Yogeshwara narrates the events of the last cycle to the Nameless-One who is "the illegitimate child" sent on a raft into the unknown at the end of the cycle. While narrating the events, Great Yogeshwara celebrates his pupil's thirtieth birthday. He is now to be sent to another similar world as another Hermit of the Mountain to stop the "endless repetition" and "the periodic disintegration" (p. 262) of the new city which is in the offing. The occasion is the beginning of a new era but the Great Yogeshwara wants to inform his pupil about the past city and the cause of its end before the Nameless-One enters the new world.

The remaining nine chapters that follow present a city governed by the Grand Master and his Ministers. The City has seven hills and people live on them according to their social status and profession which determine the geographical locations given to them on those hills. The Grand Master lives on the highest hill whereas the Ministers occupy the other hills according to their position. The middle class people live on a lower ground in pink brick buildings. The poor people including the boatmen live in an area along the river bank which is lowest in height. The Councillors of the Grand Master include the Minister of Trade, the Education Adviser, the Master of Rallies, the Astrologer, the Commissioner of Police, the Commander of the Army and General Starch who assist the Grand Master from time to time.

It can be observed that the city is obviously contemporary because it is divided in so many classes and social stratifications. This kind of class division gives birth to political trickery and the resultant conflict spoils the very health of the city. The question of allegiance raised by the Grand Master is the first step to consolidate his position. It starts the imminent conflict between the Grand Master and the boatmen. The boatmen assert their allegiance to the river because it is a question of grave importance to them because, "They consider themselves to be the children of the river, and to the river and river alone do they hold allegiance" (p. 14). It evidences that the novelist is more interested in depicting archetypes and thereby giving a mythic perspective to the novel. For the boatmen the river "is a symbol of divine mother. Of God himself" (p. 22). The boatmen are her "children" and they are ready to die for her. Further mythic perspective is added to the novel by the Grand Master's dream and the prophecy given at the very opening of the novel.

Though its meaning is obscure and ambiguous, it suggests that there is nothing final about the fate of the city. An unending debate starts between whatever is destined to occur and the will of individuals like the Grand Master who want to mould the circumstances to their advantage. The prophecy reads as follows:

> Who knows, who can read the signs,
> The workings of immortal time?
> A King I see upon a throne,
> In astronomer's grove the boatmen mourn,
> A thing of darkness growing dark,
> On city walls the shadow's mark.
> The river, I see, from a teacher rise.
> The hermit, the parrot, the teacher die.
> Under a rain the waters burn,
> To his kingdom at last the King returns.

The dream of the Grand Master is in conformity with this prophecy. For the Grand Master, his dream cannot be a faithful herald but according to the Astrologer's understanding the Grand Master's dream suggests that the present Grand Master will be the king of the city in future as he says, "yet such dreams come out of the depth of great truths and carry in them the truth of the times. If the times are troubled, the troubles must be faced. It is no secret that the city has become an unruly place, a plaything of *asuras*" (p. 15). Whatever follows later on in the novel presents the Grand Master's effort to become the king of the city. To fulfil his dream, he lets his coteries adopt ruthless measures to crush the masses when he fails to deviate them from their righteous path in spite of the tactics that he employs in the beginning.

As the first step to consolidate his position, the Grand Master with the assistance of the court Astrologer announces "The way of Three Beatitudes" in front of a large crowd. He begins with a pompous language in his introductory speech, "My children, God has sent the Grand Master to be your servant. Looking after this city is a *yajna* from him, his life is the *ahuti*...a large number of *asuras* have descended to disturb the *yajna*" (p. 7). Then he announces the way of Three Beatitudes in an ancient tongue which increases the ambiguity of his speech:

> One, the Grand Master of the city is the father and the mother of the city. All citizens are his children equally. Let them offer their allegiance to the Grand Master as a child to his father.
>
> Two, the wealth of the city belongs to everyone. However, since there are too many of us, let it be resolved that henceforth there shall be one, and only one child to a mother and two to a home.
>
> Three, while happiness and prosperity await the city and all those who follow the triple way, for him who chooses the opposite path and prefers to become a millstone round the city's neck let him be received without mercy and be treated according to...law of compassionate righteousness (pp. 17-18).

Though his speech pleases the city folk, no one understands the concept of "one child to a mother and two to a home." The "Law of compassionate righteousness" is also not very clear to them. It is only the Headman, the leader of the boatmen who understands the plot and design of these endeavours, "it had a meaning which was not apparent on the surface" (p. 18). Here it is interesting to note that the leader of the boatmen is a woman, who, by uniting the male and female principles, becomes an instrument to present the existential vision of the novel. He warns the Astrologer against such crooked announcements to befool people:

> You think that an ant is born on this earth without God's will? If it is His will that there should be only one child to a mother then surely it shall come to pass. There is no need for the Grand Master or you to pass a law... You said that the wealth of the city belongs to the people...let the city's wealth be put to use for the benefit of all (p. 20).

The announcement of "The Era of Ultimate Greatness" follows the 'Three Beatitudes' which leaves the city people with fear and foreboding. In the guise of it, the Grand Master orders the police to crush the people who have denied allegiance to him. The arrested people are taken to a prison house euphemistically called the Gold Mines. Thus the ways of a corrupt regime are adopted to arrest those people who owe their allegiance to the river. The expressions like "Three Beatitudes," "The Era of Ultimate Greatness," "Gold Mines," and "The Law of Compassionate Righteousness" are nothing but misleading euphemistic expressions. The way of "Three Beatitudes" is an enforcement of a new code of conduct for the people whereas "The Law of Compassionate Righteousness" means ruthless punishment to the unwanted people. Likewise "The Era of Ultimate Greatness" means the loss of individual freedom resulting in arbitrary arrests by which innocent people are condemned to a debased life of suffering and agony in a big underground passage which leads to a complete extinction of the soul.

To follow the mythical narrational pattern, Joshi has given mythical names to his characters who are against the rule of the Grand Master and support the boatmen. Bhumiputra, Vasu, Dharma, Shailaja and Patanjali are characters who have the courage to lead a meaningful existence along with the boatmen. The only character having a modern name is the Professor who is the teacher of Bhumiputra. All these characters are linked to the Great Hermit or the river who represents God and his divine powers. The Grand Master is always in search of these characters mainly Bhumiputra who is a teacher and is believed to be the kingpin of the conspiracy against the rulers. Bhumiputra's disappearance from the scene leads to the arrest of Patanjali.

Another attempt to gain popularity is done by the Grand Master in the form of the Festival of the River through which the Astrologer again makes an attempt to take an oath of allegiance from the people:

> In life and in death, I shall not rest, until the last of the *asuras*, the last of the conspirators, the last of the traitors is eliminated from our city and laid in the grave.
>
> In this struggle, I shall hold my allegiance to the Grand Master and to no one else. If I break this covenant, entered this day of the festival of the Great River, may the Great River curse me, strike me dead, lay waste my seed for twenty generations so help me God (p. 100).

The Grand Master follows the way of all despotic rulers. The end of the oath taking ceremony results in the coronation of Grand Master's son as the new king. First, he elevates himself by becoming the king and then he wants to ensure the succession of his son to the throne. He also creates the impression that he is obliging the country by making his son the next king. The Astrologer is Grand Master's tool and he advances attractive arguments in order to justify the identification of the Grand Master with the river. He tells the Headman, "Do not bring the Great Yogeshwara into this, Headman. All I ask is that you also swear to the Grand Master. He and the great river are one" (p. 164).

The river is an embodiment of Time and the divine mother to whom the boatmen owe their allegiance. In this eternal conflict between good and evil, those who have faith and pursue the right action acquire the affirmation of life. It is entirely left to man to choose his course of action and determine his future. The king and his men are blind to see this reality because they are devoid of faith. Even the Education Adviser who goes to the Great Hermit several times does not have this courage. The Great Hermit clarifies:

> There is nothing inevitable about the prophecy. The hand that made it believes, above all, in man's capacity to change his fate. So even if it speaks of the coming of a king, men can so conduct themselves, so choose, that the king does not come, or the king that comes is of right kind (p. 68).

A person can reach salvation in life only by profound belief in God and by following the righteous course of living. He explicates further:

> God too is a king, Minister. I am sure you have heard of him...Here, there, in you, in me, in the beggarly boatmen and his boat, in all that you see. The world belongs to God. Let him be the king of what is His (pp. 69-70).

The Education Adviser's ambition to become the king of the city has made him blind and proud like the Grand Master. Due to his shrewd mentality he is far from understanding the eternal truths put forth by Great Yogeshwara who develops into the most prominent archetypal symbol in the novel.

The next chapter "The Lottery Stall" depicts the increasing opposition against the Grand Master. The Professor and Shailaja's brother use Bhoma's parable about the naked king to expose the moral nakedness of the Grand Master. The hollow character of the system is revealed to the people and they think that they "had been lulled into sleep and were now awakening to their surroundings" (p. 127). They have awakened only after much harm has been done. The rule of the Grand Master has a corroding impact on the souls who are struggling against their extinction. Dharma's father sees a hole in his chest, "It had started one morning when shaving before a mirror, he thought he saw a hole in his reflection" (p. 133). When he asks his friend he says, "It is Three Truths Syndrome, Stasis of the soul. Atrophy of the brain and locomotor functions" (p. 135). It is a clear picture of what man becomes when cruelty, corruption, violence, hypocrisy, deception and material benefits dominate the society. Both the Great Yogeshwara and the Nameless-One are "instruments...of the great God...who is the Master of the Universe." They are sent with a mission to purify the city of its "egoism, selfishness and stupidity" (p. 263) which have taken the city in their grip.

The next chapter "The Return of the Teacher" brings Bhumiputra into action. The Great Hermit meets him and tells Bhumiputra that he is just a tool in the hands of God. Bhumiputra works as a teacher and a guide to the boatmen and becomes a mouthpiece of the novelist to present his Hindu existential vision. Lord Krishna talked about *Jnana Yoga* in the context of body and soul and impressed upon Arjuna that the ultimate reality is soul because it never dies. The *Bhagvadgita* preaches that "wise men do not grieve for the dead or for the living" (Radhakrishnan: 102). A man who practises *Jnana yoga* treats "pleasure and pain, gain and loss and victory and defeat" (*Ibid*: 114) alike. Bhumiputra inspires the boatmen with a similar vision:

> For if you are afraid to die then your soul is already dead and the great river, your mother, cannot help you even if

> she were back from the dungeons of the shadow...if you choose the death of your soul above the death of your body, then no one, man or god, can help you (p. 146).

Further Master Bhoma inspires them with a similar vision of the immortality of their soul:

> The guns can kill your bodies, yes. Are you then afraid to die?...What is man, howsoever powerful! That he so fills you with dread, that you let him come between you and your understanding...What do you choose, then this wisp of the mist or the great river herself? (p. 146).

Though Master Bhoma advises and invites them to revolt against the Grand Master, he is himself afraid and says, "the thought of the Grand Master's prisons fills me with dread...I have done my bit and cannot go on" (p. 155). The Great Hermit encourages Master Bhoma like Lord Krishna where he asks Arjuna to shun all the worldly considerations and adopt the way of *Dharma* and *Kartavya*:

> The city, this world, all this is the manifestation of the One, and not the shadow of the Grand Master's ego, as the Grand Master might imagine. And it is He, the one without a second, who secretly supports and guides all that you see, and what you do not see (p. 156).

It is the Will of God according to which the world runs. Great Yogeshwara further explains the role of man in the plan of the Universe and the value of individual choice:

> But the Almighty can manifest through men only what men allow Him to manifest. This is why men and cities and nations must choose. There is the upward path that leads to freedom and there is a downward path that, for the moment at least, must lead to perdition (p. 156).

The doctrine of *Karma* tells us that man's final growth rests with himself because his future is not pre-determined. Reïterating the importance of individual choice, Sartre realised that man may choose to be "nothing" like a "table" or may "choose to reach above the stars" (Kaufmann: 47). The *Upanishads* much before Sartre have insisted that a man can break with the past through concerted will and action. Man's growth rests on his way of living and thus he is not an insignificant unit of the universe but an active agent and it is only through his actions that he can achieve his personal salvation as well as collective salvation. Likewise the people of the city must decide their course of action in future from the two options open to them.

The prison houses euphemistically called Gold Mines are a part of the *maya* (*Sansara*) which like a labyrinth destroys man's capacity to think and confuses him so that he fails to choose the path of affirmation. The Professor and the Headman are put in those 'dark dungeons' where any thought of self and affirmation is gradually dissolved in the darkness. Plunged into suffering and torture they bear all the injustice inflicted upon them by the rulers. The Headman is blinded by them and the Professor goes on fast until his death to oppose the despot, The Grand Master. The Great Hermit claims all these happenings a part of his *yajna* to purify this world:

> This *yajna* of mud people, Patanjali, burns only on sacrifice. When the fire is low, when the flame is dying, men must feed it with their own lives. And who knows, the gods now call for the professor's life? Who knows this be the great purpose that they have reserved for him? (p. 166).

The death of Professor becomes a matter of grave concern for the Grand Master and to project a clean image, he orders the release of all prisoners. The issue of such a decree is followed by another order by the Grand Master, "No prisoner was to be set free unless he proves his innocence" (p. 172). For Master Bhoma, "the decree was further evidence of the contempt in which the Grand Master held the inhabitants of the city" and it "was not worth the paper it was written on" (p. 174). The news of Professor's death and the sad plight of the Headman results in the strike of the boatmen leading to a complete disruption of river transport in the city. Further dragnets are launched to suppress the boatmen and the mud people. The conflict between the boatmen and the police reach its zenith signifying the conflict between good and evil. Due to internal rivalries and a secret deal between the Education Adviser and the Minister of

Trade, the shock Brigades which consist of students and teachers join the boatmen and give the Commissioner a humiliating defeat. A second Deed of National Partnership is signed between the Army and the Minister of Trade to support the candidature of the Minister of Trade for Grand Mastership of the city. Thus, it is clear that the city has reached its hour of crisis and the administrative machinery of the city is cracking slowly.

The ultimatum given by the Commissioner to the boatmen proves to be futile. The Headman tells the Colonel, "The boatmen are also committed to die to the last man" (p. 207) and advises the boatmen to fight for their freedom:

> There are perhaps other ways to fight this, but we do not know of them. It is an ancient evil that has come out of the Seven Hills. So, let the boatmen fight it in their ancient way. The beast we now face is deaf and blind and is set on a single purpose, the Astrologer's oath. The king that was naked is naked still. Death, I say, is preferable to surrender to the king (p. 208).

He tells Bhumiputra about the inevitable death which awaits everyone at the appointed hour, "Death is certain for all and here is a reason to die. As I told you, the course of our struggle is set. Let it run" (p. 208). Thus the crisis which has enveloped the city gets bleaker and alarming. The Grand Master calls the members of the Supreme Council and after much deliberations over the caste and heredity factor in the choice of a king, they select the Grand Master as the King and the Minister of Trade as the new Grand Master.

The circumstances of the city suggest to the Great Hermit that there is no time left to mend. He puts the same question to the river: "What should I do?... Is there still time? Is there hope? Is there a point?" (p. 216). He opens the city's horoscope and sends it to the court Astrologer for further interpretation:

> Astrologer, I send you my greetings. What I send you herewith you will doubtless recognize. The wheel has nearly come full circle. The hour of God is upon us and the time is short. As you had hoped, a king now sits on the throne. My death and the death of the teacher are certain...I beg of

> you to once again consider the meaning of the line we have so long disputed. I beg you to bring both the interpretations to the knowledge of the king. Let him choose...More than the future of a king, Astrologer, what is involved here is the future of a city, a civilization. I hope you will not misunderstand. And now, farewell-till, in another birth we meet again (p. 217).

The Astrologer realises his fault but the Grand Master is devoid of any faith in God: "And God—what is God? Where is He? Does he even exist? He must surely have other things to worry about than intervene in the affairs of this city where we in any case now rule" (p. 219). For the Great Hermit, it is not difficult to guess the future of the city. All the three wings of the forces are brought into action by the Grand Master with their modern weapons; helicopters, gunboats, commandos, laser beams and tanks which crush Master Bhoma, Dharma and others who are so determined to preserve themselves from corruption and trickery.

While this suppression goes on, a change in the river is noticed by the Great Hermit, "The sky had once again become overcast. The clouds hung low and they were black. More clouds were rolling in from the horizon. Below him the river was rising" (p. 227). The river continues to rise with a music of drums and engulfs each and everything in the city in its domain, "To the melody now other notes are added, and the sound of drums and instruments of which man has no knowledge" (p. 251). For the Grand Master and his allies, the river becomes an identity of horror and awe, "all of a sudden the river was not a river any more.... The inmates of the palace shuddered in horror as the new Grand Master's building broke in the middle and flood by floor, frame by frame, fell into the sea. One last wave uprooted the foundations and sent them flying into the sky" (p. 257). All of them perish in the river water and Great Yogeshwara ends the story of the city and its king saying:

> For seven days and seven nights it rained without a stop. On the eighth day the sun rose and from a clear sky stared

> down at a vast sea of water. The sea was calm and gave no hint of the agitation that had gone into its making. Of the Grand Master and his city nothing remained (p. 260).

Thus the river which is an embodiment of Time (p. 129) becomes almost "the primordial sea" and wipes out everything and through her the Eternal or Divine reasserts itself. The city has met its end but it is not an end. A new city has to emerge on its ruins. The Great Yogeshwara tells the Nameless-One:

> On the ruins of that city, as always happens a new city has risen. It is ruled by another Grand Master, which, of course, need not always happen. In the new city is another Professor, another Bhumiputra, another tribe of boatmen. There is another council and another set of councillors. The men have other names but the forces they embody remain unchanged. And into all this when you go you will, perhaps, be known as another Hermit of the Mountain. And it is possible you will have a disciple whose name will be Little Star (p. 262).

The end of the novel is full of optimism and hope for affirmation as we see Great Yogeshwara sending his disciple to teach people the significance of prayer, faith and understanding to the new city:

> "The main thing is to prevent this endless repetition, this periodic disintegration. But to achieve that we need purity."
> "Purity?"
> "Yes the city must purify itself if it is not to dissolve again."
> "Purity itself of what?"
> "Of egoism, selfishness, stupidity" (p. 263).

The negation of these weaknesses is a pre-requisite to self-knowledge which brings understanding and unfolds the truth. Understanding brings commitment to pursue the righteous path with full vigour and faith in God. Though it is not easy but one must try as Great Yogeshwara says: "The question is not of success or failure; the question is of trying...The city must strive once again for purity. But purity can come only through sacrifice" (p. 263). The novelist thus explores the very foundations of faith and right action. The significance of God to man is shown by The Great Hermit and he affirms God as "the highest Truth"; He is "the noblest thing each of us can imagine" (p. 70) and "belief in God restores peace to human soul" (p. 76). It is not success that we always get because "in any case we are only instruments...of the great God in the highest heaven who is the master of the universe...His is the Will, His is the Force" (p. 264).

When we observe the mythic perspectives and archetypes other than the city and the river, the Great Yogeshwara and the Nameless-One have different mythical associations. The Great Yogeshwara is the "Puran Purush" and his pupil, the Nameless One suggests Manu on the raft at the time of *pralaya*. Other semblances make us believe that the Great Yogeshwara is Lord Krishna telling his pupil the gospel of *Dharma* and revealing to him the mystery of the world and of Himself. The concluding verse of *Gita* names Lord Krishna as Yogeshwara and he is the one who watches this '*leela*' (play) very minutely. The Nameless-One is Arjuna, who is hesitant at first, but proceeds to undertake the assignment after being enlightened. Both the Yogeshwara and the Nameless-One are "instruments of great God in the highest heaven who is the master of the Universe" (p. 264). This suggests Lord Krishna's *avatara* in human form when the Lord chooses to enter into His own world.

The Nameless-One is also a messiahnic figure like Christ. He is an "illegal" child but he is the chosen one. Running parallel to these archetypes is the symbol of the great mother—the river. The boatmen are her "children" and they are ready to die for her. The great river speaks to her children whenever they are in trouble. The Professor often goes to her to seek her advice. The Professor is like a Bhisma-figure seeking help from his mother Ganga in *The Mahabharata*. The river sustains the city like a protecting mother and destroys the city when it becomes too overbearing. It is on her bossom that a child is born to the Great Yogeshwara so that he is properly instructed and sent to yet another city as its saviour. The Hermit of the mountain is the saviour of human race because his timely action saves the Nameless-One who is to be sent to the new world. The child that he selects is the chosen one. The Hermit performs the *yajna* to erase the blasphemy of the Astrologer and calls the child to pour "*Ahuti*" in the Hermit's "*yajna*" near the river. When the Nameless-One is sent as a future Hermit, it indicates the psychological rebirth of the Great Hermit.

Another factor which adds the mythic perspective to the novel is the repeated sound of music and drums whenever something crucial happens in the novel. This music is heard at the start of the novel when Great Yogeshwara is preparing the Nameless-One for his quest:

> And when he had drained the cup the Nameless-One felt as vast as the sky and as tall as the mountain, and there came into his ears, as though from beyond the stars, the sound of a melody played on one string. The music rose and fell and grew in volume and was joined by the sound of dancing feet. And presently, the music and the dancing filled the infinite spaces of the cosmic night (p. 11).

This sound of drums and music is heard intermittently in the novel to the last when the city is being submerged in the disastrous river:

> The music rising to a shattering volume, fills the four quarters of the sky. The notes leap from one pole to the other, awesome yet playful. To the melody now other notes are added, and the sound of drums and instruments of which man has no knowledge. And now another wind rises and there is the sound of dancing whirling feet and of laughter (p. 251).

All these musical notes and dancing suggest the dance of Lord Shiva and awaken the reader to the universal stage on which the action of the novel is moving on. All these ethos transcend the contemporary into the cosmic and the transient into the timeless. The devastation of the city by the primordial waters of the river is a sort of cleansing of an impure, selfish and faithless creation and it is replaced by another world full of hope and affirmation.

According to Jean Paul Sartre, Man as an individual should preserve the authenticity of his self without taking refuge in "Bad Faith" (Grene: 265). It is a matter of individual choice for human beings to lead an authentic existence which Sartre regards as an absolute virtue in Existentialism. This absolute virtue is wholly different from mere adjustment with the surroundings as Marjorie Grene opines: "The concept of authenticity is not a concept of adjustment—in fact with respect to the current ideal of the well-adjusted member of society, it is truly and deeply a heresy" (*Ibid*: 270). When we see the individuals of the city from this angle, the elite Ministers and Councillors practise "Bad Faith" because they are conscious of the wrong they are doing, but they still continue doing so complying with the Grand Mother's orders. The middle classes who live in the colony of the brick houses never protest and thus they lack authenticity. Quite opposite to these people are Dharma and his father who are high officials in the Grand Master's administration. When they realise the loss of their authenticity Dharma begins to imagine himself a boatman and dresses himself like them whereas his father becomes a complete wreck when he observes a hole in his body. It is only the poor boatmen who have the courage to lead an authentic existence though they pay a heavy price for it. Grand Master's father had once cautioned him regarding their honesty and courage:

> They are not as simple as they seem.... They consider themselves to be the children of the river, and to the river alone do they hold allegiance. They believe, unfortunately, with their hearts, and for their beliefs they are willing to die. And don't let their poverty mislead you into believing that they can be bought (p. 14).

Man's liberty is completely thwarted nowadays due to different threats in the environment as well as by death which is the irrevocable certainty and only few individuals are brave enough to face them. For Heidegger, "genuine existence is existence which dares to face death" (Grene: 266). In this respect the boatmen boldly safeguard their authenticity in Heideggerian sense. Their Headman (a woman) is the symbol of strength and commitment and she very well understands that the secret of man's life is his liberty to choose. As Sartre says: "For the secret of a man is not his Oedipus Complex or his inferiority complex: it is the limit of his own liberty, his capacity for resisting fortune and death" (*Ibid*: 274). A representative case of the authenticity of the mad people is the old man, Patanjali. He is arrested as a substitute of Bhumiputra (Master Bhoma) because Bhoma is not apprehensible. When he is asked by Dharma to apologize if he wants to be set free, he replies: "But why should I apologize? I have done no wrong. Rather the Grand Master should apologize for making such absurd rules" (p. 26). Likewise Bhumiputra, the Professor and Dharma's grandfather also preserve their authenticity. The Grandfather grows unique roses on his farm in a city which is barren and he is yet another person to oppose the will of the rulers. Ultimately, all these people die in the extensive attack launched by the armed forces.

The political scenario employed by the novelist serves as a background as well as it lends contemporaneity to the happenings of the novel. Absurdity, anarchy, alienation are some of the characteristic features of existentialism which are seen rampant in the city. There are shopping arcades, cigars, newspapers, lottery stalls, card-clubs, radio waves and conveyors that work on electricity. The weapons which are employed to crush the people include self-loading rifles, tanks, helicopters and lasers. The city has its class divisions as well as co-existence of different ways of life according to which people live on different geographical locations in the hills.

The Indian political scenario of the Emergency is in many respects paralleled in the novel. There is a despotic ruler (Grand Master) who imposes his decisions on other people though there is an outward appearance at the top where he is supposed to be elected by his councillors. He has a Rallies Master to organize rallies in his support to give the impression that he is popular among the city folk. The Minister of Trade proposes in the meeting of the "Supreme Council" that he be made King and argues that it is in the interest of the people. He says:

> I shall briefly put forward certain criteria that the king of the city should meet. First, as already decided, he must be a wearer of sacred thread. Second, he must come from a family which has already demonstrated its willingness to make sacrifice for this city. Third, he must command the affection of our masses and the trust of the armed forces

> and the business class. Fourth, he should be above the petty squabbles of the bazaar.... Now gentlemen, the only person who meets these criteria is our beloved Grand Master. I propose, therefore, that he be requested to accept the onerous burdens of the king's high office (p. 213).

The Rallies Master, the Minister of Trade and others are all subservient to the status and will of the Grand Master. Indian Emergency also had legislatures and judiciary though they were totally subservient to the chief of the executive. To enforce his laws, the Grand Master uses all kinds of suppression with the help of guns and by the use of army and the police, though the army and the police are kept to protect the city from external and internal aggressions. The euphemistic declarations and decrees by the Grand Master meet the Twenty Point Program followed by a strict control of media and the satellite (p. 173). The Rallies Master is made to organize rallies so that people may form the impression that the Grand Master and his son are very dear to the masses, as the Rallies Master tells the journalist: "And now, journalist, I must gather rallies not only for the Grand Master but his son as well. The city must now face its final humiliation and I must be an instrument to it" (p. 76). The Grand Master regulates an impractical family planning, "One, and only one, child to a mother and two to a home" (p. 18) which seems to be taken from the happenings of Emergency in India. Further a straightening of roads is done by the use of bulldozers devastating the houses of hundreds of people who live there because the Grand Master's wife wants it to be so for no reason other than of having a nicer view. She says: "How much nicer would the view be if there were a straight road running from here to the river" (p. 37). Later on those people are allowed to stay at the same place, now called "Avenue Asthough" as if their houses were still there. There are references to money power (p. 90), hoarding (p. 93) and adulteration of oil (p. 153). The conversation between the Minister for Trade and Pinstripe suggests how even the Government officials are involved in raising the price of commodities:

> Prinstipe went on: "In the light of the approaching Festival of the River cooking oil can bring in excellent revenues.

> Prices can be pushed very high if the produce of the Gold Mines is cornered."
>
> "I shall do what I can do" (p. 64).

The suffering and torture to which people are subjected in the Gold Mines is also contemporary. They are sent to prison without a trial in the court of law. Later on the Grand Master instructs the Astrologer to issue a decree but has no intention to implement it as the present day leaders befool people by promising big things but doing just the opposite in practice. This can be seen when the Grand Master tells the Astrologer:

> "Yes, Astrologer, let us decree that all prisoners shall be told their crimes, or set free."
>
> "Issuing a decree, Astrologer, does not mean its immediate implementation" (p. 167).

In order to accomplish his motive, the Grand Master gives ministerial posts for political reasons irrespective of talent and potentials. In the present circumstances of power politics where so many parties are involved, it has become a major issue which dominates the formation of any government. In order to keep the shock brigades away from joining hands with the boatmen the Grand Master appoints the Education Adviser to the Council. As the Little Star tells the Professor: "When the Grand Master inaugurated the New Era the Astrologer advised him to appoint the Education Adviser to the Council. That was the only way of keeping his shock brigades from joining hands with the boatmen" (pp. 35-36). This Education Adviser has nothing to do with education, talent and capability. The only thing he has is the support of students and teachers, whose support the Grand Master wants to win.

Further contemporaneity is provided to the novel when the Grand Master imposes restriction on the freedom of the press and does not let any independent newspaper flourish. The Little Star informs the Professor:

> There are two newspapers in this city. One of them is owned by a trust of which the Astrologer is the head. The other is owned by a girl. The girl is five years old and

cannot manage a newspaper. It is managed for her by the Master of Rallies. The Master of Rallies also controls the satellite. The satellige controls the radio and the video. The Master of Rallies controls the satellite on the Grand Master's behalf because the satellite is the private property of the Grand Master (p. 88).

The impact of Gandhian thoughts can be traced in the activities of the Great Yogeshwara, the Headman and Bhumiputra. The Hermit never incites anyone for a rebellion but tries to the last extent to persuade the Grand Master and his allies to learn by themselves:

> God resides as much in a Grand Master as in you and me. Is not therefore always room for hope? We never know when the soul of a Grand Master is touched and in that hour his life is transformed (p. 263).

For the upliftment of the whole society every individual has to be purified. Once this is done, the "endless repetition," "the periodic disintegration" (p. 262) will be pervented and a stable society will come in existence. All this meets the Gandhian vision to achieve Ramrajya by resistance and service. The Hermit advises the Minister of Trade not to be ambitious but to defy the Grand Master and expose him, because "A man aspiring to rule this city must first learn to be the slave of this city" (p. 113). The echoes of Marxism are also discernible in the novel when Bhumiputra advises the Boatmen:

> Brother and sisters, the pyramids, the palace, the Seven Hills, deaf though they now be to the boatmen's cries, it is by the sweat of the boatmen's brow that such things are built. And it is by the sweat of the boatmen's brow that brick mansions are raised, and avenues laid, and avenues made straight, and the armour of the soldier bought. It is by your sweat, my brothers, that the wealth of this city is produced. And now, I say to you, you will refuse the shameless phantoms the sweat of your brow, the skill of your hands (p. 178).

By presenting politics in the novel in an allegorical way Joshi succeeds in transcending its contemporaneity because the novel contains characters who are archetypes rather than recognisable human beings with individual characteristics. It is remarkable to see that the novelist succeeds in providing a message to us without the psychologically realized characters. When the prophecy and the statements of Great Yogeshwara are observed minutely, there is a kind of controversy in them. It is suggested that the incidents that are happening in the city are destined to occur according to the prophecy so the persons who are involved in it cannot be blamed. If the Grand Master is believed to be a tool in the hands of destiny, he cannot be blamed of having realized his ambition at the cost of people's liberties because the prophecy claims the coming of a king: "A King I see upon a throne," and it clearly asserts that the Grand Master is just a play thing and Fate has chosen him to be that way. The Astrologer says: "Grand Master, the time has come to let you know that there exists a prophecy that speaks of the coming of a king. Your dream is the herald that we have been waiting for" (p. 15). As it is foretold in the prophecy that "A thing of darkness growing dark/On city wall's the shadow's mark" (p. 216) it can be understood that the king is bound to be ruthless and oppressive. If the Grand Master is a phenomenon then it is not his own fault but it can be the fault of his chair which corrupts him. If everybody behaves in the same manner as this Grand Master has behaved, then the present Grand Master who has made him king cannot be regarded as guilty. A person can only be blamed if he chooses the absurd path himself. He must have his free will to choose between allegiance to God or to man like the boatmen.

The City and The River thus does not constitute a departure from Joshi's interest to explore the existential predicament of man but goes one step further in suggesting man's metaphysical reconciliation as an answer to all his worries, agonies and alienation. He affirms the relevance of God to man in his life: "Here, there, in you, in me, in that beggarly boatman and his boat, in all you see and you do not see, the world belongs to God" (p. 70). The final message of the novel is summed up in the Great Yogeshwara's words: "His is the Will, His is the Force" (p. 264) and so an unquestionable faith in God and surrender to Him is the only solution to our threatened existence. *The City and The River* by its theme and execution proves that Joshi has been deeply influenced by the Hindu existential vision and the novel continues the spiritual quest of his earlier novels through measured rhythms of myths, legends and archetypes. By the time we reach the end of the novel, we feel like completing a quest and it is a universal human quest for affirmation through negation of self. The question is not of individual success or failure but of collective efforts for the common good. Joshi's obsessive preoccupation with man and his situation is his *forte* and he has explored its staggering variety with rare perspicacity and acumen.

WORKS CITED

Greene, Marjorie. "Authenticity: An Existential Virtue," *Ethics*. 62, 4 (July 1952).

Joshi, Arun. *The City and The River*. New Delhi: Orient Paperbacks, 1994. All Further citations refer to this edition followed by paginations.

Kaufmann, Walter. *Existentialism: From Doestoevsky to Sartre*. Cleveland and New York: Meredian Books,The World Publishing Co., 1968.

Prasad, Madhusudan. "Arun Joshi" in his (ed.), *Indian English Novelists: An Anthology of Critical Essays*. New Delhi: Sterling, 1982.

Radhakrishnan, S. (ed. & tr.). *The Bhagvadgita*. New Delhi: Harper Collins Publishers, 1993; rptd. 2000

Rao, M. Madhusudan. "The Hindu Existential Concern in Arun Joshi's Fiction," A.R. Rao & M. Sivaramakrisna (ed.). *When East Meets West*. New Delhi: Sterling, 1994.

7

Overall Evaluation

The foregoing analysis of Arun Joshi's novels demonstrates that he has been preoccupied with the problem of twentieth century man's dilemma and its repercussions. In an age when religious faith is fast disappearing and man feels culturally uprooted and socially alienated on account of his own (mis)doings, the message of serious artists like Joshi is most welcome and called for. In fact the gravity of spiritual crisis coupled with material affluence has created an unprecedented situation where cynicism has blurred the long cherished values of life. For lack of an intuitive discipline implanted in an affirmative attitude to the macrocosm and its happenings, modern man seems convinced of the purposelessness of his existence and its activities. Joshi's protagonists represent a cross-section of humanity and this lends an authentic aura to his creative world.

That Hinduism attaches utmost value to the 'right way to live' and enjoins upon its followers to lead a responsible life is a commonplace of Indian spiritual discipline. Barret even goes to the extent of regarding it as the only concern of oriental wisdom:

> ...for the oriental, the only reason for bothering with philosophy is to find release or peace from the torments and perplexities of life.... Philosophy is the soul's search for salvation...deliverance from suffering and evils of the material world (Barret: 5).

And Joshi has candidly confessed his debt to Indian scriptures as extensively deliberated upon in the preceding pages. The journey of his heroes can be treated, to borrow a religious terminology, as a movement from 'becoming' to 'being,' from initial negation to final affirmation. In fact the truncated state of the protagonists is a first step towards the preparation for their metaphysical reconciliation and its resultant poise. They subject themselves to all kind of purgatorial experiences obviously trying to discover the secret of life in their distinctive ways in accordance with their individual accomplishments and angularities.

Joshi's first three novels viz., *The Foreigner, The Strange Case of Billy Biswas* and *The Apprentice* deal with three ways of redemption as preached in *The Bhagavadgita*, the *Karmayoga*, the *Jnanayoga* and the *Bhaktiyoga* respectively. Being orphaned at an early age, Sindi Oberoi, the hero of *The Foreigner*, develops an atheistic attitude to life and its problems. The unfortunate circumstances toss him from one set of blows to another and he appears to be wearied of his existence. His chance meeting with a catholic priest whose teachings are identical to a Vedantin's—"all love—whether of things, or persons, or oneself—was illusion and all pain sprang from this illusion" (Joshi, 1968: 145)—marks a turning point in his career and he is prompted to accept the concept of *Karmayoga*, redemption through action without attachment. His subsequent joining the Khemka's firm on his visit to India provide him an opportunity to execute his realisation. By deciding to help the labourers in the factory and in their struggle of existence, he reaches the stage of affirmation, "sometimes detachment lies in actually getting involved" (Joshi, 1968: 188).

The Strange Case of Billy Biswas presents its protagonist as one who debunks the futility and imperfection of civilized society where sensitive persons are invariably inclined to feel alienated. Billy's instinctive yearning for a meaningful life makes him a psychological case since he feels restive in an environment uncongenial to leading a life of peace and serenity. The process of dissatisfaction gets completed when he seduces Rima Kaul, "It gradually dawned upon me that a tremendous corrupting force was working on me. It was as though my soul was taking revenge on me for having denied it for long that other thing, that it had been clamouring for" (Joshi, 1971: 187). While in Sindi's case it was his meeting with a spiritual man that marked a change in his personality, in Billy's case it is otherwise. His headlong plunge into sensual pleasures opens his inner eye and he is in a position to make up his mind to move into a primitive world to seek his personal salvation and affirmation of the 'other thing' in his life—"that other thing was, and is, after all, what my life is all about" (Joshi, 1971: 187). Such realisation tantamounts to redemption through knowledge, *Jnanayoga* which dispels all false impressions about the reality of human situation.

The concept of salvation through devotion, *Bhaktiyoga* has been powerfully exemplified through the story of Ratan Rathor in *The Apprentice*. The novel's main thrust is on the purification of the soul and also on the abiding values of humility and self effacement in human life. The protagonist plans his life full of hope and ambitions and subjects himself to all pettiness but all expectations turn out to be otherwise. The realisation that "one's life has been a total waste" (Joshi, 1974: 135) that dawns upon him after his friend's death goads him to undergo penance. Ratan starts from the very lowest by dusting the shoes of the congregation outside the temple every morning like an apprentice with a desire "to learn." The way which Ratan chooses for his purification meets the vision of *Bhaktiyoga* which informs that the purification of self is not to be obtained by any ritual, or dogma but by service to mankind and prayer to God. Such an apprenticeship in humility arms man to face the challenges of life successfully.

Joshi regards this world as a labyrinth, an intricate maze where man has to carve his way out for himself. That this is an extremely trying proposition is depicted in *The Last Labyrinth*. The thematic structure of the novel concentrates upon two coordinates—'hungers of the body' and 'hungers of the spirit.' The protagonist Som Bhaskar's odyssey shows that he is torn between the diverse pulls of the spirit and the body. Life is so full of distractions like lust, greed, wrath and pride which serve as different layers of a labyrinth that man is most likely to get deviated from the right path of salvation. Should a man be sceptical by temperament, he is in for greater trouble as Som's responses to the situation of his life suggest. Lal Haveli, the locale of the novel itself is literal as well as metaphorical in its implications and serves as a fitting symbol of the world outside. All attempts undertaken by Anuradha and Gargi to bring a meaningful change in Som's way of life ultimately prove futile on account of his inbuilt suspicious nature and this only proves *Gita*'s well-known dictum—*sanshayatma vinashyati* (a doubting Thomas is doomed to perish).

Joshi's last novel *The City And The River* treats the tussle between 'allegiance to God' and 'allegiance to Man' as a recurring phenomenon in human history. Through its narrator the Great Yogeshwara the novelist brings forth the myth of *sristi* and *pralaya* and by implication satirises the alarmingly materialistic nature of existence. The novel seems to create the impression that the mundane values have started a war against the river which stands for peaceful and etherial aspect of the macrocosm. It would not be a far-fetched analogy to infer that in such a situation William Wordsworth might reiterate "The World is too much with us.../ Little we see in Nature that is ours...." Unlike his earlier novels where the story revolves round the protagonists, the two main characters in *The City And The River* viz., the Great Yogeshwara and the Grand Master represent two sets of values, as if they were the two options either of which man may choose in accordance with his perception of reality. The modifiers 'Great' and 'Grand' also suggest the quality of approach the two principal characters show in their conduct and activities. There are echoes of *The Bhagavadgita* in the narrator's exposition that "this city, this world, all this is the manifestation of the One, and not the shadow of the Grand Master's ego" (Joshi, 1990: 133). He further explains:

> But the Almighty can manifest through men only what men allow Him to manifest. This is why men and cities and nations must choose. There is the upward path that leads to freedom and there is the downward path that, for the moment at least, must lead to perdition (*Ibid*: 156).

It is remarkable that Joshi views money as a corrupting force throughout his novels. Be it Sindi Oberoi of *The Foreigner*—"America is a place for well-fed automations rushing out in automatic cars. I'd go mad if I had to do that" (Joshi, 1968: 76) or Billy Biswas of *The Strange Case*—"I sometimes wonder whether civilization is anything more than making and spending of money" (Joshi, 1971: 92). They are equally critical of and fed up with their apparently comfortable situations. Ratan Rathor of *The Apprentice* coming as he does from an impoverished family has his own attractions for material success which ultimately lands him into trouble. However he comes to realise towards the close "My soul has killed. You put yours to pawn. But souls that were pawned could perhaps be retrieved" (Joshi, 1974: 140). The hero of *The Last Labyrinth* Som also reckons that material gains cannot necessarily bring solace to man.

The issues taken up by Joshi hammer on the consciousness of his readers about their own choice between the materialistic values and spiritual affirmation. His novels suggest that man's metaphysical reconciliation is the only answer to all the agonies of his existence. They demonstrate that modern man may overcome his sense of uprootedness by self searching and introspection. Their instinctive yearning for affirmation and authenticity is a native cultural thrust which most defines Indian metaphysical concerns. The protagonist reaches a critical point where he is in utter confusion, and then encounters a catastrophe which becomes the basis for his introspection and prompts him ultimately to reconcile to the world. The Great Yogeshwara's exhortation has its own logic behind it:

> ...let not fear sow confusion in your heart. Whatever happens the Lord will not forsake you, nor will your work be fruitless. Be rest in peace. Be not afraid. All shall be well (Joshi, 1990: 157).

Such kind of faith meets the Kierkegaardian thought of "a metaphysic of hope" as well as the Hindu existential vision which is essentially affirmative in character. A sensitive reader can identify himself with Joshi's protagonists and scrutinise for himself the relevance of his daily struggles fraught with unnerving propositions. The significance of Joshi's creative output lies not simply in the number of volumes he has brought out, but in the quality of their authentic responses to dilemmas that have been baffling humanity since the Fall.

WORKS CITED

Barret, William. *Irrational Man*. New York: Doubleday and Co., 1962.

Joshi, Arun. *The Apprentice*. New Delhi: Orient Paperbacks, 1974; rptd. 1993.

——. *The City And The River*. New Delhi: Vision Books, 1990; rptd. 1994.

——. *The Foreigner*. New Delhi: Hind Pocket Books, 1968; rptd. Orient Paperbacks, 1993.

——. *The Last Labyrinth*. New Delhi: Orient Paperbacks, 1981.

——. *The Strange Case of Billy Biswas*. New Delhi: Asia Publishing House, 1971.

Select Bibliography

PRIMARY SOURCES

Novels by Arun Joshi

The Apprentice. New Delhi: Orient Paperbacks, 1974; rptd., 1993.

The City And The River. New Delhi: Vision Books, 1990; rptd. 1994.

The Foreigner. New Delhi: Hind Pocket Books, 1968; rptd. New Delhi: Orient, 1993.

The Last Labyrinth. New Delhi: Orient Paperbacks, 1981.

The Strange Case of Billy Biswas. New Delhi: Asia Publishing House, 1971.

Miscellaneous Writings

"The Sri Ram Group," *Illustrated Weekly of India*. New Delhi, May 30, 1971.

The Survivor. New Delhi: Sterling, 1975.

Lala Shri Ram, A Study in Entrepreneurship and Industrial Management, New Delhi: Orient Longman, 1975.

"The Only American From Our Village," Madhusudan Prasad (ed.), *Contemporary Indian English Stories*. New Delhi: Sterling, 1984, 64-70.

"Towards Finding An Expression," R.K. Dhawan (ed.) *The Fictional World of Arun Joshi*. New Delhi: Classical Publishing Company, 1986, 15-16. (with Khushwant Singh)

Sri Ram: A Biography. New Delhi: Asia Publishing House, 1968.

SECONDARY SOURCES

Abraham, Joy. "Arun Joshi's Novels: The Absolute Without A Name," his (ed.) *A Critical Study of Novels of Arun Joshi, Raja Rao and Sudin N. Ghose*. New Delhi: Atlantic Publishers and Distributors, 1998, 18-67.

Abraham, Joy. "Narrative Strategy in The Strange Case of Billy Biswas." Dhawan, *The Novels of Arun Joshi*, 191-200.

——. "The Foreigner: A Study in Techniques." Dhawan, *The Novels of Arun Joshi*, 143-61.

——. "Vision and Technique in The Apprentice." Dhawan, *The Fictional World of Arun Joshi*, 210-22.

Abraham, P.A. "Patrick White's Voss and Arun Joshi's The Strange Case of Billy Biswas: A Comparative Note on a Journey into the Interior." *Literary Criterion* 27.4 (1992): 22-30.

Alam, Qaiser Joha. "The Image in Arun Joshi's Fiction." *Language and Literature*, 33-44.

Amur, G.S. "New Parable," *Indian Literature*, 34-4 (July-Aug. 1991, 152-157.

Asnani, Shyam M. "A Study of Arun Joshi's Fiction," *The Literary Half-yearly*, 19, 2 (July 1978), 41-49.

Awasthi, Kamal H. & Lalit, M. Sharma. "The World of 'Outsiders' in *The Foreigner and Voices in The City*," A.K. Singh (ed.) *Contemporary Indian English Fiction*. New Delhi: Creative Books, 1993, 104-14.

Bande Usha. "Anita Desai, Arun Joshi and Anasakti Yoga." Language Forum 14.1 (1988): 54-64.

——. "Archetypal Patterns in The City and the River." Dhawan, *The Novels of Arun Joshi*, 257-64.

——. Arun Joshi's Women: An Esoteric Experience," Naresh K. Jain (ed.) *Women in Indo-Anglian Fiction: Tradition and Modernity*. New Delhi: Manohar Publications, 1999, 128-40.

——. "Post-Colonial Anxiety in the Novels of Arun Joshi," Surya Pandey (ed.), *Writing in a Post-Colonial Space*. New Delhi: Atlantic Publishers and Distributors, 1999, 77-86.

——. "Symbolism in Arun Joshi's The Lost Labyrinth." ed. Srivastava, R.K. *Symbolism*, 150-62.

——. "Victor-Victim Syndrome in Arun Joshi's The City and the River." *Victim Consciousness*, 106-13.

Bannerji, Purabi. "A Winner's Secrets," *The Sunday Statesman*. Calcutta, Sunday 27 Feb., 1983, 4.

Bano Hamide. "The Quest for True Self in Arun Joshi's The Foreigner." *English Studies in India* 3 (1988): 112-22.

Barret, William. *Irrational Man.* New York: Doubleday and Co., 1962.

Benihal Arup. "A Stylistic Insight into The Last Labyrinth." Dhawan ed. *The Novels of Arun Joshi,* 230-40.

——. "The City and the River: A Critical Review." Dhawan, ed. *The Novels of Arun Joshi,* 274-75.

Bhatnagar, M.K. *The Novels of Arun Joshi : A Critical Study,* New Delhi : Atlantic Publishers and Distributors, 2001.

Bhatnagar, O.P. "Arun Joshi's The Foreigner," *Journal of Indian Writing in English,* 1.2 (1973): 9-14.

——. "The Art and Vision of Arun Joshi." Scholar Critic 4.6 (1984): 30-43.

——. "Arun Joshi's The Foreigner," *The Journal of Indian Writing in English,* I, No. 2, July 1973, 9-14.

——. "Woman Characters in the Novels of Arun Joshi." *Commonwealth Review* 6.1 (1994-95): 155-58.

——. "Arun Joshi's The Foreigner: A Critique of East and West," *The Journal of Indian Writing in English,* 1.2 July, 1973.

Bree, Germaine. (ed.) *Albert Camus: A Collection of Critical Essays.* New York: O.U.P., 1968.

Camus, Albert. *The Fall.* Harmondsworth: Penguin Books, 1968.

——. *The Myth of Sisiphus.* Harmondsworth: Penguin, 1975.

——. *The Outsider.* Harmondsworth: Penguin, 1973.

——. *The Rebel.* Penguin, 1973.

Chandar, K.M. "The Quest of Faith in Arun Joshi's *The Last Labyrinth," The Indian Novel in English,* ed. R.N. Sinha and R.K. Sinha. Ranchi: Ankit Publisher, 1987.

Chandra, Suresh. "The High Culture Fiction of Arun Joshi and Uma Vasudev," *Culture and Criticism.* Delhi: B.R. Publishing Corporation, 1987.

——. "Towards Authenticity: A Study of The City and the River." Dhawan, *The Novels of Arun Joshi,* 265-73.

Chandran, M.V.R. "*The Strange Case of Billy Biswas,*" *The Deccan Herald.* 31 Oct., 1971, 6.

Chingre, C.D. "Contrast as Technique in Arun Joshi's *The Strange Case of Billy Biswas,*" *The Indian Journal of English Studies,* Vol. XXX (1991-92).

——. "Women Characters in The Novels of Arun Joshi," *Commonwealth Quarterly.* 6, 1 (1996), 155-58.

Cruickshank, John. *Albert Camus & The Literature of Revolt.* New York: O.U.P., 1960.

Damodar, G. "The Outsiderist Tradition in Joshi and Desai." *Kakatiya Journal of English Studies* 13 (1993): 59-66.

Darryl, D. Monte. "*The Strange Case of Billy Biswas,*" *The Times of India.* 26 June 1971, 5.

Daruwalla, Keki N. "Review of *The Last Labyrinth,*" *Indian Literature.* 26, 4 (July-Aug 1983), 136-40.

Das, R.J. "Moral Dilemma in Arun Joshi's *The Apprentice,*" *Journal of Literature & Aesthetics* (March 1981), 11-17.

Devi, P. Janaki. "Search for Identity in the Novels of Arun Joshi." *Journal of English Studies* (Warangal) 10.1 (1978): 620-27.

Dhawan, R.K. (ed.) Exploration in Modern Indo-English Fiction. New Delhi: Bahri Publications, 1982.

——. *The Fictional World of Arun Joshi.* New Delhi: Classical Publishing Company, 1986.

——. *The Novels of Arun Joshi.* New Delhi: Prestige, 1992.

Dua, M.R. Joshi's Reply to M.R. Dua, September 3, 1971.

Dutta, Padma. "Problem of Individualism: A Critique on Arun Joshi's Use of Symbols and Archetypes in *The Last Labyrinth,*" *Journal of Indian Writing in English.* 18, 1 (Jan., 1991), 31-40.

Dwivedi, A.N. (ed.). "The Novels of Arun Joshi: A Critical Study." *Studies in Contemporary Indian Fiction in English.* Allahabad: Kitab Mahal, 1987.

Flaherty, Wendy O. *Hindu Myths.* Harmondsworth: Penguin, 1978.

Funk and Wagnals, *Standard Dictionary of Folklore, Mythology and Legend.* New York: Harper Bros., 1984.

Gautam, Hansa. "Tension and Tonicity in Arun Joshi's Novels." *Contour* 1.2-3 (1992): 10-15.

Ghosh, T.K. *Arun Joshi's Fiction: The Labyrinth of Life.* New Delhi: Prestige Books, 1996.

Gopalkrishnan, M.G. "The Short Stories of Arun Joshi." *Arun Joshi—A Study of his Fiction,* (ed.) N. Radhakrishnan. Madurai: Scholar Critic, 1984: 68-73.

Grene, Marjorie. *Introduction To Existentialism.* Chicago: The Univ. of Chicago Press, 1970.

Gupta, G.S. Balarama (ed.) *Studies in Indian Fiction in English.* Gulbarga: JIWE Publications, 1987.

Guruprasad, Thakur. "The Lost Lonely Questers of Arun Joshi's Fiction." Dhawan, *The Fictional World of Arun Joshi,* 155-66.

Hegde, M.G. "Arun Joshi's *Lala Shri Ram*: A Study," *The Journal of Indian Writing in English.* (Jan., 1989), 18-22.

——. "Distance and Discovery as Techniques: A Study of the Narrative Strategy of *The Strange Case of Billy Biswas.*" *Osmania Journal of English Studies* 25 (1989): 92-100.

Heidegger, Martin. "An Introduction To Metaphysics," (tr.) R. Nanheim. New York: Doubleday and Co., 1961.

Ionesco, Eugene. "Dans Les armes de la Ville," *Cahiers de la Campagne Madeleine Renaud* (tr.), E.B. Ashton. New York: O.U.P., 1956.

Iyengar, K.R.S. *Indian Writing in English.* New Delhi: Sterling Publishers, 1962; rptd. 1996.

——. "The Fiction of Arun Joshi," *The Humanities Review.* 3, 2 (1982), 39-40.

Jain, Jasbir. "Foreigners and Strangers: Arun Joshi's Heroes," *Journal of Indian Writing in English.* 5, 1 (July 1975), 52-57.

JamKhandi, Sudhakar R. "Arun Joshi: An Emerging Voice in Indian English Literature," *The Literary Endeavour.* 6, 1-4 (1983), 36-44.

Jaspers, Karl. *Man In The Modern Age.* New York: Doubleday and Co., 1956.

Jeewan, Parawathy. "Towards Authentic Selfhood: Concept of Freedom in the Novels of Arun Joshi," *The Quest.* 12, 1 (1999), 32-38.

Jha, Mohan. "*The Foreigner*: A Study in Innocence and Experience." Dhawan, *The Fictional World of Arun Joshi* 168-175.

Joshi, Surender. "Point of view and Theme in Arun Joshi's *The Strange Case of Billy Biswas.*" Saxena, *Glimpses* Vol. 3. 70-79.

Kalinnikova, Elena J. "In Search of Anti-Hero: Anita Desai and Arun Joshi." Kalinnikova *Indian English Literature : A Perspective,* 174-78.

Kaufman, Walter. *Existentialism: From Doestoevsky to Sartre.* New York: Meridian Books, 1968.

Kher, Indra Nath. "The Archetypes of Love and Death in Arun Joshi's *The Last Labyrinth,*" *Journal of Indian Writing in English.* 2, 1-2 (Jan.-July 1992), 53-66.

Koller, John M. *The Indian Way.* New York: Macmillan, 1982.

Krishnamma, B.G.R. "*The Strange Case of Billy Biswas,*" *The Hindu.* 11 July 1971, 8.

Kumar, Shiv. "Autobiography of a Lost Soul." *The Tribune,* Bombay, 19 Dec. 1981, 4.

Kumar, Sunaina. "A Tribute: Arun Joshi and His Extraordinary Obsessions." *Indian Book Chronicle* June 1993: 20.

Kumar, T. Vijay. "Allegory, Negation and History: Arun Joshi's *The City and The River,*" Vinay Kirpal (ed.) *The Post-Modern English Novel: Interrogating the 1980s and 1990s.* New Delhi: Allied Publishers, 1997, 145-52.

Lal, P. "Myth and The Indian Writing in English: A Note," M.K. Naik (ed.) *Aspects of Indian Writing in English.* Madras: Macmillan, 1972, 15-26.

MacIver, Robert M. *The Ramparts We Guard.* New York: Macmillan, 1950.

Macquarrie, John. *Existentialism.* Harmondsworth: Penguin, 1972; rptd. 1986.

Marcel, Gabriel. *The Existential Background To Human Dignity.* New York: Harper Bros., 1969.

Mathai, Sujata. "I am a Stranger to My Books." (Interview), *The Times of India.* (Bombay), Sunday, 10 July 1983, 8.

Mathur, O.P. "Arun Joshi and The Gita." Pathak, *Indian English Fiction* 132-45.

——. "The Contemporary and The Cosmic in Arun Joshi's *The City and The River*," Yaravintelimath (ed.) *New Perspectives.* 1996, 147-53.

——. "*The City and The River*: A Leap into Eternity," K.K. Sharma (ed.) *Points of View*, 2, 1. Ghaziabad: K.K. Publications, 1993, 61-72.

——. "Survival and Affirmation in Arun Joshi's Novels," *Modern Indian English Fiction.* New Delhi: Abhinav Publications, 1993.

Mathur, O.P. and G. Rai. "The Existential Note in Arun Joshi's *The Strange Case Of Billy Biswas* and *The Apprentice*," *Commonwealth Quarterly*, 5, 3 (December 1980), 26-30.

——. "From Existentialism to *Karmayoga*: A Study of Arun Joshi's *The Foreigner*," A.K. Srivastava (ed.) *Alien Voice.* Lucknow: Print House, 1981, 107-15.

Mazumdar, Shubhra. "A Commentary on The Times." *The Times of India.* 24 Feb. 1981, 8.

Meitei, M. Mani. "*The Strange Case of Billy Biswas*: Awareness of Worlds Within Worlds," *The Quest.* 4, 2 (1991), 19-20.

——. "Indian Ethos in Arun Joshi's *The Last Labyrinth*," R.K. Pathak (ed.) *Indianisation of Indian English Literature.* New Delhi: Bahri Publications, 1994, 160-72.

Mohan, Devinder. "Arun Joshi: *The Foreigner.*" *Major Indian Novels and Evaluation*, (ed.) N.S. Pradhan. New Delhi: Arnold Heinemann, 1985, 174-91.

——. "Beyond the Litany of Wants: Contexts of Arun Joshi's Fiction Towards *The Last Labyrinth*," Vinay Kirpal (ed.) *The New Indian Novel in English: A Study of The 1980s.* Delhi: Allied Publishers, 1992, 82-90.

——. "The Dance of the Life and Death: Arun Joshi's Fiction." *Asia Week* 16 Aug. 1987.

——. "The Image of Fire in Arun Joshi's *The Strange Case of Billy Biswas.*" Dhawan, *The Fictional World of Arun Joshi.*

Mohan, Devinder. "The Language of the Splinterred Mirror: The Fiction of Arun Joshi." R.K. Dawan (ed.), *Commonwealth Fiction*. New Delhi: Classical Publishing Co., 1988, 17-32.

Mohanty, Mahendra Kumar. "Filial Relationships in *The Foreigner*" Dhawan, *The Novels of Arun Joshi,* 115-21.

Mukherjee, Meenakshi. *The Twice Born Fiction: Themes and Techniques of The Indian Novel in English*. New Delhi: Arnold-Heinemann, 1974.

Murchland, B. *The Age of Alienation*. New York: Random House, 1971.

Nagarajan, S. "An Indian Novel," *Considerations,* (ed.) Meenakshi Mukherjee. Bombay: Allied, 1977.

Naik, M.K. *Dimensions of Indian English Literature*. New Delhi: Sterling Publishers, 1985. F.P. 1984.

——. *A History of Indian English Literature*. New Delhi: Sahitya Akademi, 1982.

Narasimhaiah, Sanjay. "Arun Joshi's *The Last Labyrinth." Literary Criterion* 15.2 (1981): 81-89.

Nietzsche, F. *Thus Spake Zarathustra* (tr.) A. Tille and M.M. Bozman. New York: Dutton, 1933.

——. *The Joyful Wisdom* (tr.) Thomas Common, Macmillan, 1910.

Padma, T. "Problem of Individuation: A Critique on Arun Joshi's Use of Symbols and Archetypes in *The Last Labyrinth,*" *Journal of Indian Writing in English*. 18, 2 (1984), 33-40.

——. "Crypto-Myth and Metanovel; Arun Joshi's *The City and The River*: An Appraisal," *Framing Literature,* 1996, 107-15.

Pandey, Lala Udai Bhan. "Anita Desai and Arun Joshi: A Comparative Study," R.K. Dhawan (ed.) *Commonwealth Literature,* 1 (1989), 224-26.

Paranjape, Makarand. "Lost in the Labyrinth," *The Times of India*. New Delhi, 24 Feb. 1991, 8.

Pathak, R.S. "Arun Joshi's Novels: An Indeterminate Search for Meaning in Life." *Scholar Critic* 4.6 (1984).

——. *"The Indo-English Novelists' Quest for Identity," Explorations in Modern Indo-English Fiction,* (ed.) R.K. Dhawan. New Delhi: Bahri Publications, 1982.

Pathak, R.S. "The Alienated Protagonist in the Indo-English Fiction," Glimpses of Indo-English Fiction, Vol. I (ed.) O.P. Saxena. New Delhi: Jainsons Publications, 1985.

——. *Indian Fiction in English: Problems & Promises.* New Delhi: Northern Book Centre, 1994.

Pathania, Usha. "Having and Being: A Study of *The Foreigner.*" Dhawan, *The Novels of Arun Joshi:* 133-42.

——. "The Quest for Being: An Analysis of *The Foreigner.*" Kaul & Jaidev, 159-166.

Piciucco, Pier Paolo. "An Interview with Arun Joshi," *The Journal of Indian Writing in English.* 25, 1-2 (1997), 87-97.

——. "Fictional Technique and Rhetorical Devices in Arun Joshi's *The Apprentice." Literary Criterion* 34.2 (1999): 30-43.

Prabhakaran, M.S. "The Apprentice: An Overview." *Scholar Critic* 4.6 (1984).

Prasad, Ch. A. Rajendra. "After the Fall: A Critique in Arun Joshi's *The Apprentice," Revaluations,* 2, 1 (1997), 79-85.

Prasad, Hari Mohan. *Arun Joshi.* New Delhi: Arnold-Heinemann, 1985.

—— "The Crisis of Consciousness: A Thematic Analysis of *The Last Labyrinth." Scholar Critic* 4.6 (1984).

——. "Dimensions of Realism in Indo-English Fiction," *The Indian Journal of English Studies,* XXI, (1981-82).

Prasad, Madhusudan. (ed.) *Indian English Novelists: An Anthology of Critical Essays.* New Delhi: Sterling Publishers, 1982.

——. "Cornering Arun Joshi: A Critical Perspective on *The Last Labyrinth." Scholar Critic* 4.6 (1984).

——. "Arun Joshi," *Indian English Novelists: An Anthology of Critical Essays,* 210-16.

Prasad, V.V.N. Rajendra. "Arun Joshi: Self as Labyrinth." Prasad, V.V.N 108-29.

——. "*The Apprentice:* Self as Labyrinth." Dhawan, *The Novels of Arun Joshi,* 210-16.

——. *The Self, The Family and Society in Five Indian Novelists: B. Rajan, Raja Rao, Narayan, Arun Joshi, Anita Desai.* New Delhi: Prestige, 1990.

Prempati, D. "*The Strange Case of Billy Biswas:* A Serious Response to a Big Challenge." Dhawan, *The Fictional World of Arun Joshi,* 176-85.

Radha, K. "From Deatchment to Involvement: *The Foreigner*" Painker, *Contemporary India Fiction in English,* 81-90.

——. "Fugitive for Self and the City in Margaret Atwood's *Surfacing* and Some Indian Novels in English." Begum 21-32.

Radhakrishnan, N. (ed.) *Arun Joshi—A Study of his Fiction.* Gandhigram, Madurai: Scholar Critic Publication, 1984.

——. "The Women Characters of Arun Joshi." *Scholar Critic* 4.6 (1984).

Radhakrishnan, S. (ed. & tr.) *The Bhagavadgita.* New Delhi: Harper Collins Publishers, 1993; rptd. 2000.

——. *Eastern Religions & Western Thought.* New Delhi: O.U.P., 1974.

——. (ed. & tr.) *The Principal Upanisads.* New Delhi: O.U.P., 1989.

Raizada, Harish. "Double Vision of Fantasy and Reality in Arun Joshi's Novels." Dhawan, *The Fictional World of Arun Joshi,* 69-103.

Ram, Atma. "Arun Joshi," his (ed.) *Interviews With Indian English Writers.* Calcutta: Writer's Workshop, 1985, 61-64.

Rama, R.P. "Arun Joshi's *The Foreigner—A Review," Indian Writing Today,* July-September, 1970.

Ramakrishna, D. "Academics and Yogis: Reflections on The Recent Indo-English Fiction," *The Journal of Indian Writing in English,* 7, 2 (July 1979), 89-96.

Rangachari, S. "T.S. Eliot's Shadow on *The Foreigner," Arun Joshi; A Study of his Fiction,* (ed.) N. Radhakrishnan. Madurai: *Scholar Critic,* 1984.

Rani, Rekha. "The Language of Dreams in *The Last Labyrinth.*" Dhawan, *The Novels of Arun Joshi,* 224-29.

Rao, C. Malathai. "The Foreigner," *Literary Criterion,* 8, 4 (1969), 76-77.

Rao, M. Madhusudan. "The Hindu Existential Concern in Arun Joshi's Fiction," A.R. Rao & M. Sivaramakrisna (ed.) *When East Meets West.* New Delhi: Sterling, 1994, 149-61.

Reddy, V. Gopal. "From Alienation to Community: A Note on The Novels of Arun Joshi," *Kakatia Journal of English Studies.* 7 (1985-86), 87-96.

——. "The Apprentice: An Existential Study." *Kakatiya Journal of English Study."* 5 (1983): 9-16.

Ross, Robert. "The Clash of Opposites in Arun Joshi's *The Last Labyrinth." Literary Criterion,* 25, 2 (1991), 1-9.

Rushdie, Salman. "Reclaiming a City and a History," *Express Magazine* (*The Indian Express*), 11, March 1984.

Sartre, Jean Paul. *Being and Nothingness: An Essay on Phenomenological Ontology.* (tr.) Hazel Barnes. New York: O.U.P., 1966.

——. *Existentialism & Humanism* (tr.) Philip Meret as *The Mentor Philosophers.* New York: O.U.P., 1955.

——. *Nausea.* (tr.) R. Baldick. Harmondsworth: Penguin, 1965.

Satpathy, S.C. "From Passivity to Awareness: A Study of the Narrator-Protagonist in Arun Joshi's *The Apprentice." Journal of Literary Studies* 2.2 (1979): 121-32.

Satyanarayana, E. "Towards Affirmation: A Reading of Arun Joshi's 'A Trip For Mr. Lee.' and 'Survivor'." Narendra Kumar, V.L.V.N. *New Perspectives,* 108-112.

Sharma, Brahma Dutt. "The City and the River as a Political Novel." Dhawan, *The Novels of Arun Joshi,* 241-56.

Sharma, D.R. "Arun Joshi and His Reflective Insiders." *Literature: East and West.* 11, 1-4 (Jan-Dec 1997): 100-11.

——. "The Fictional World of Arun Joshi." *Indian P.E.N.* 43, Sept.-Oct. 1977. 1-5.

Sharma, Shyam Sundar. "The Two Worlds in *The Last Labyrinth."* Dhawan, *The Fictional World of Arun Joshi,* 240-48.

Sharma, Susheel Kumar. "Philosophical Reverberations in *The Foreigner."* Dhawan, *The Novels of Arun Joshi.* 122-32.

——. "*The Strange Case of Billy Biswas*: A Psycho-graph of an Alienated Hero." Dhawan, *The Novels of Arun Joshi.* 62-116.

Singh, Khushwant. "Arun Joshi." *Hindustan Times,* 24 Jan. 1981: 6.

Singh, R.S. "Aloneness Alone: Anita Desai and Arun Joshi." Singh R.S., *Indian Novel in English,* Arnold Heinemann, 1977: 164-78.

——. *Indian Novel in English: A Critical Study.* New Delhi: Arnold-Heinemann, 1977.

Srinath, C.N. "Arun Joshi's *The Apprentice:* The Novel of Our Times" Narendra Kumar V.L.V.N., *New Perspectives* 113-17.

——. "Crisis of Identity: Assertion and Withdrawal in Naipaul and Arun Joshi," his (ed.) *The Literary Landscape.* Delhi: Mittal Publications, 1986, 81-92.

——. "Native Roots and Novel Foliage: An Understanding of the Achievement of Indian Fiction in English." *Literary Criteria* 21.1-2 (1986): 60-85.

——. "The Fiction of Arun Joshi: The Novel of Interior Landscape," his (ed.) *The Literary Landscape,* 40-69.

Srivastava, K. Ramesh. "The Theme of Alienation in Arun Joshi's Novels." *Ken: A Journal of English Studies* 1(1982): 13-23.

——. "Intricate Alleys in Arun Joshi's *The Last Labyrinth,*" K.N. Awasthi (ed.) *Contemporary Indian English Fiction.* Jallandhar: A.B.S. Pub., 1993, 83-91.

Srivastava, Narsingh. "Quest for Truth and Identity in Arun Joshi's *The Last Labyrinth,*" R.S. Pathak (ed.) *Quest for Identity in Indian English Writing.* Delhi: Bahri Publications, 1 (1981), 80-86.

Tilak, B.G. *Srimad Bhagavad Rahasya.* (tr.) B.S. Suktankar. Poona: Aryabhusan Press, 1965.

Tripathi, J.P. "From Raju to Billy: Changing Aspects of Selfhood," R.S. Pathak (ed.) *Quest for Identity in Indian English Writing,* 1 (1981), 75-80.

Venkateswara Rao, J. "*The Foreigner:* An Existential Dilemma." *Triveni* 64. 1-2 (1995): 73-76.

Venugopal, C.V. and M.G. Hedge. "Soul's Progress from Innocence to Knowledge: A Study of *The Apprentice.*" *Kakatiya Journal of English Studies* (Warangal) 8 (1987-88): 163-69.

Verghese, C. Paul. *Problems of Indian Creative Writers in English*. Bombay: Somaiya, 1971.

Verma, K.D. "The Metaphysics and Meta Structure of Appearance and Reality in Arun Joshi's *The Last Labyrinth." International Fiction Review* 21.1-2 (1994): 44-50.

——. "Alienation, Identity and Structure in Arun Joshi's *The Apprentice." Ariel* 22.1 (1991): 71-90.

Vijaya Kumar, T. "Allegory and the Negation of History: Arun Joshi's *The City and the River."* Kirpal, *Postmodern Indian English Novel,* 145-52.

Walter, Inna. "Arun Joshi's Vision of Life, Love, God and Death in *The Last Labyrinth,"* G.S. Balaramagupta (ed.) *Studies in Indian Fiction in English*. Gulburga: JIEW Publications, 1987, 46-52.

Wandrekar, Kalpana. "The Foreigner: Chaos of Cultural Confusion." Wandrekar 79-91.

Yadav, Kumkum. "The Importance of Being Billy—Victim(s) in Arun Joshi's *The Strange Case of Billy Biswas."* Bande, *Victim Consciousness,* 94-105.

Zachner, R.C. *The Bhagavadgita*. London: O.U.P., 1989.

Reviews

Bandopadhyay, Manohar. Rev. of *The Strange Case of Billy Biswas. Patriot* 1 Aug. 1982.

D'Monte, Darryl. "A Hollow Rebel." Rev. of *The Strange Case of Billy Biswas. Times of India* 27 June 1971: 10: 5-7.

Futehally, Laeeq. "Story-Telling." Rev. of *The Apprentice and The Survivor. Quest* 93, Mar.-Apr. 1975: 93-94.

Hariharan, Gita. "A Political Parable." Rev. of *The City and the River. Indian Literature* 144 (1991).

Iyengar, K.R.S. "The Fiction of Arun Joshi." Rev. of *The Last Labyrinth. Humanities Review* 3.2 (1981): 39-40.

Keating, H.R.F. Rev. of *The Last Labyrinth. Times Literary Supplement,* 6 Aug. 1982: 863.

Malathi Rao, C. Rev. of *The Foreigner. Literary Criterion* 8.4 (1969): 76-77.

Mathai, Anna Sujatha. "In Search of Meaning." Rev. of *The Last Labyrinth. Indian Book Chronicle,* 16 June 1983: 219-20.

Mazumdar, Shubra. Rev. of *The City and The River. Book Review* Jan.-Feb. 1991: 28.

Mukherjee, Meenakshi. Rev. of *The Foreigner. Quest* 60, Sep.-Oct. (1969): 101-03.

——. Rev. of *The Strange Case of Billy Biswas. Quest* 72, Sep.-Oct. 1971: 121-24.

N.B. Rev. of *The Foreigner. Opinion Literary Quarterly* (India) 1 (1974): 50-52, 54.

——. Rev. of *The Strange Case of Billy Biswas. Opinion Literary Quarterly* 1 (1974): 50-52, 54.

Naikar, Basavaraj S. Rev. of *The Last Labyrinth. World Literature Today* 56.4 (1982): 752-53.

R.S. Rev. of *Apprentice. Divine Life* (India) 12 Oct. 1975: 19.

Rao, K.S.N. Rev. of *The Strange Case of Billy Biswas. Books Abroad* 46.4 (1972): 726.

——. Rev. of *The Apprentice. Books Abroad* 49.1 (1975): 185.

——. Rev. of *The Apprentice. Times of India,* 25 June 1976: 10.

——. Rev. of *The Foreigner. Times of India,* 17 Sep. 1972: 9.

——. Rev. of *The Foreigner. Thought* 24, 15 July 1972: 18-19.

——. Rev. of *The Foreigner. Indian and Foreign Review,* 15 July 1969: 21-22.

——. Rev. of *The Last Labyrinth. National Herald* (Sunday) 22 Nov. 1981: 4.

Saraiya, Indu. Rev. of *The Apprentice. Indian P.E.N.* 41.8 (1975): 4-16.

Shettigara, Tina. "Entering the Maze." Rev. of *The Last Labyrinth. CRNLE Review Journal* 1 (1982): 53-54.

Tonpe, Vaijayanti Savant. Rev. of *The City and the River. Seminar* 384 Aug. 1991: 48.

Trivedi, Harish. "The Bitch Goddess." Rev. of *The Last Labyrinth. Book Review,* Sep.-Oct. 1982: 72-74.

Dissertations

Abraham, Joy. "Themes and Narrative Techniques in the Novels of Arun Joshi." Calicut U, 1991.

Bhuyar, R.S. "Arun Joshi: A Study of His Fiction." Amravati U, 1985.

Dubey, Amitabh. "Thematic Patterns and Structural Design in Arun Joshi's Novels." Dr. H.S. Gour U.

Hegde, Manjunath Gajanan. "Arun Joshi: A Study in Theme and Technique." Karnatak U, 1991.

Joshi, P.S. "Themes and Techniques of Arun Joshi's Novels." Diss. (M.Phil.). South Gujarat U, 1985.

Navaneethan, S. "Thematic Progression in the Novels of Arun Joshi." Bharathisadan U, 1985.

Pradhan, Shanta. "Modern Element in Indian English Fiction with Special Reference to the Novels of Raja Rao, Anita Desai and Arun Joshi." Gauhati U, 1990.

Prasad, V.V.N. Rajendra. "Self, Family and Society in the Novels of Rajan, Raja Rao, R.K. Narayan, Arun Joshi and Anita Desai." U of Krishnadevaraya, 1988. New Delhi: Prestige Books, 1990.

Rajendra Prasad, Chiliki Appala. "The Function of 'Enigma' in Arun Joshi's Novels." Andhra U, 1990.

Ranveer, P. Rukmani. "Encaged Sensibility in the Novels of Arun Joshi." Kakatiya U, 1990.

Satyanarayana, N. "New Morality in Indian-English Fiction with Special Reference to Anand, Narayan and Arun Joshi." Kakatiya U, 1987.

Index